ne·gro·phi·li·a

ne·gro·phi·li·a

From Slave Block to Pedestal ~
America's Racial Obsession

by Erik Rush

WND Books

NEGROPHILIA
WND Books

Published by WorldNetDaily
Washington, D.C.

WRITTEN BY ERIK RUSH
JACKET DESIGN BY MARK KARIS
INTERIOR DESIGN BY PAULINE NEUWIRTH, NEUWIRTH & ASSOCIATES, INC.

WND Books are distributed to the trade by:
Midpoint Trade Books
27 West 20th Street, Suite 1102
New York, NY 10011

WND Books are available at special discounts for bulk purchases. WND Books, Inc.
also publishes books in electronic formats. For more information,
call (541-474-1776) or visit www.wndbooks.com.

First Edition

ISBN: 978-1-935071-82-2

Library of Congress information available

Printed in the United States of America

10 9 8 7 6 5 4 3 2

acknowledgments

I would like to humbly acknowledge my family, for putting up with me; Bill and Bob and their crew; and Bruce and Eleanor Oyen, for their moral and technical support.

contents

foreword

Uncle Tom.
Oreo.
Race traitor.
Black white boy.
Bitch-ass nigger cracker.

WHAT PRECEDES ARE but a few of the epithets that have been directed toward me as a result of the sociopolitical commentary I've written that has focused on race and race politics.

Those were actually the *milder* ones.

Don't feel sorry for me, though; at least I have the consolation of knowing I'm right.

You heard me. You see, when I was a child, my parents taught me that racism, bigotry, and discrimination were not acceptable, no matter who was practicing them. This was important to them since they were an interracial couple and I was a mixed-race child. So, I applied what I'd been taught. Strangely, the nation around me evolved into one that would adopt its own subjective view—not only of what was and was not racism, bigotry, and discrimination, but also of what was and was not right and wrong.

At this juncture, we still live in a land in which we have freedom of speech and, therefore, a right to be wrong. Consequently, I have no qualms as regards making the discernment that the sort of folks who employ the type of invective I opened with, and those who validate them, are horribly *wrong*. They are not simply people who "have their opinion too"; they are as *wrong* as the people Rev. Dr. Martin Luther King Jr. marched against during the last century. As such, they should have no reasonable expectation that their retrograde views ought to be taken into account in a free society, *regardless of what their own race happens to be*. This is an all-important distinction.

For around a quarter to one-third of all adults in the United States, the mythology surrounding black Americans that has been cultivated over the last forty years is sacrosanct. For them, criticizing or questioning its veracity is like denying the Holocaust. Hence the reactions.

I used to wonder what would cause people's passions regarding such topics to drive them to a descent into the crudest, most hateful of vitriol. In truth, it more resembles the sort of things we used to hear from uneducated, white segregationist protesters in days gone by. The extent of this passion is something with which I simply cannot identify. Sure, I've been angry enough to curse someone out, even angry enough to harm someone, but this was either due to basic human fallibilities (such as immaturity) or a direct threat of life or limb to myself or someone who I cared about. In the case of most people, I think that the capability for, or inclination toward, rash speech wanes with age, emotional maturity, or spiritual grounding.

Concerning people I find to be the most threatening to our society and way of life, I am sometimes markedly frustrated at their ignorance, arrogance, or blatant self-interest. I would rather they didn't have the sway that they do. Yes, I would like to see them disenfranchised. However, I don't believe that ad hominem attacks or yearnings for harm to befall those with whom I disagree are of any use whatever.

Perhaps that aforementioned immaturity is the key. My experience has been that those who engage in these verbal assaults are dedicatedly aligned with political factions that have marked proclivities toward ad hominem attacks. They don't respond—they react. Their arguments are typically emotional, their logic poorly formed, and their comportment typically rather base. Pertaining to the type who takes exception to my point of view, there is also something else to factor in: those who encourage them, and for whom it is an imperative to promote enmity toward people with my point of view.

I suppose these are, as they say, issues for another time—or another book.

A lot of people are going to hate my guts for writing this. Some will go as far as to say that this is itself a racist, "anti-black" book, that it seeks to "undo" forty years of progress in the area of race relations and civil rights. Some will no doubt take up the mantle of armchair psychoanalysts and claim (as many have previously) that I have "identity issues" as a black man, that I'm self-loathing and so forth. Some will dismiss it out of hand. Ignore it and it will—*please, God!*—go away.

Others will hit the warpath . . .

While I quite expect all of this, it will neither negate the truths contained herein nor the intellectual dishonesty that abounds apropos the subjects of race relations and race politics in America.

So, they can continue to call me a race traitor, wholly unmindful of the racism in that very statement. They can accuse me and people of my convictions of being hateful, ignoring the abject hatred in nearly every statement they utter. They can, by their diatribes, continue to expose the absolute darkness of their minds and their souls, leaving me with naught to do but pray that they never breed.

But enough about me . . .

Few are telling anything even remotely resembling the truth as regards the politics and dynamics of race relations in America. If deception and propaganda abound at this juncture in our history— as they most assuredly do—the area of race politics is shot through with it like no other. Part of the reason for this is the nature of the issue and how it has evolved. In 1964, there was justifiable collective anger on the part of black Americans, and justifiable collective shame on the part of whites.

If human sensitivities were amplified, however, during the Civil Rights Movement of the 1960s due to the dismantling of Jim Crow, desegregation, and the resistance to same, they have been even more intensified by activists: whites who suffer from an inordinate amount of residual guilt ("guilty whites"), the press, and the advent of political correctness (or, to put it more aptly in Orwellian terms, Newspeak and Thoughtcrime).

American culture, and so our nation, has had aspects of running to extremes. As Britannia went from ruling the waves to waiving the rules, America appears to be following the same suit in terms of its sociology (as well as its foreign policy). Moving from repressive to dangerously bohemian, from exclusive to imprudently indiscriminate in little more than a hundred years, Americans seem to have been unable to see the middle ground, let alone put on the brakes as they passed through. Regarding the lot of blacks in America, they have gone from being relegated to a status resembling that of the *dalits* (untouchables) of India to being perceived as almost angelic in their infallibility, despite their human frailties being as evident as that of any other ethnic group.

Unfortunately, people tend to believe what they want to believe, particularly in these days of potent ideology, well-honed propaganda, and its efficient delivery systems. The parts of this book that would defuse arguments regarding the validity of the thesis will be glossed over by people who habitually form conclusions that are emotionally based or rooted in ideological zealotry. They will come to these conclusions regardless of logic.

For decades now, Americans have been sold a bill of goods regarding those of us of African (or mixed) descent, other ethnic minorities, and race relations in general. That bill, tragically, contains the worst kind of intellectual excrement. White guilt is still encouraged, despite unprecedented opportunities for blacks in America. Black multimillionaires assert in the press that we live in a racist nation in which blacks are still oppressed—and millions nod mutely in agreement. Arguments for reparations to black people for slavery—a logical travesty as well as a horribly inequitable proposition—are still proffered with regularity and seriously considered by many Americans.

As life has increasingly imitated art—here I refer to the portrayal of blacks and trends in the entertainment media—the perception of blacks on the part of non-black Americans has become increasingly tainted by the aforementioned media, propaganda of the establishment press, activists, and politicians. While this may have led to a coexistence of inquisitiveness, it has also imparted a pernicious, counterfeit understanding of blacks on the part of non-black people as well as an inordinate deference toward blacks, particularly among whites. Black people themselves continue to suffer from this phenomenon because it discourages social and intellectual accountability on their part.

Why do these conditions exist, how did they come about, and what—if anything—can be done to neutralize them? That is what this book will answer.

There is a distinct possibility that this book will inspire the full wrath of the far left, and the politically active black community in particular. These will consider this book an obscenity; lemming-like, many blacks, never having read it, may gather in throngs to pour their scorn upon this book and its author. This will all be well and good, as it will serve to gauge the reach of this information. More than bringing this subject to light, I believe that exposing what the power brokers in this nation—black leaders among them—have done to stultify the productivity, intellect, and spirit of blacks at large is even more important. My aim here is to inform all Americans, regardless of race, hopefully to a degree sufficient to effectively kick a very essential leg out from under the far left's malevolent platform.

Many psychologists and clergy hold that human beings utilize all sorts of things to fill the "hole" where spiritual enlargement ought to reside. Some people adopt religious zealotry itself, mistaking it for spirituality; others adopt extreme vanity, work, or vices. Still others use political zealotry and civil activism, which become as beloved and sacrosanct as another's faith. To question such a person's convictions is like slandering Islam's Muhammad or asserting to an evangelical Christian that Christ was not the Son of God. It can evoke inordinately explosive reactions. The concepts within this book will fall within the parameters of such a challenge and, thus, will very probably be perceived as just that sort of threat or offense.

As I indicated, among the criticisms of this book will likely be the claim that it seeks to reverse or overturn forty years of progress in the area of civil rights. Such a charge will be moronic, since it is highly unlikely that this author would profit in any way from a return to affairs as they stood in pre–Civil Rights Movement America. But the charge may be made nonetheless. What would be desirable, rather, would be a *lateral* move in the area of civil rights and race relations, in which advancement occurred, but the perversion of politics and personal agendas were prevented from taking a toll. Such an accomplishment could also be a stride toward pulling down America's accursed secular-socialist framework.

I hope that black Americans read this book. Obviously, I hope that a lot of people read it. Selfish motives aside, if a significant number of black people read this book, open-minded ones will be enlightened. Perhaps some will even take it as a call to action against those who have been exploiting them (quite a few of whom are also black), in the name of equality, for the last few decades. Maybe they will join with their white neighbors and turn their ire toward those who really seek to enslave us all. If whites read this book, maybe fewer will be afraid of speaking the truth with reference to purveyors of the aforementioned intellectual excrement.

If you happen to be among the black folks I mentioned in the opening paragraphs, or perhaps a zealous white progressive who'd like to boil me in a cauldron of flaming oil right about now, all I can say is that it's doubtful this book will change your mind about anything. If you believe that *The View* is a television program that reflects the American majority perspective, that Jesse Jackson is a righteous man, and that Barack Obama is a great leader, then you're set in your beliefs; logic and evidence generally do not tend to neutralize the volatile reaction initiated when sacred tenets of one's doctrine are criticized.

You can seethe all you like. I don't mind the invective, I don't scare easily, and I'm certainly not going to fret over what the brainwashed think or say. If you happen to fit into this unfortunate category, bristling with arrogance and vapid certainty, you are *the fool who follows.* You are the kid who jumped off of the Empire State Building just because your friend did.

Happy landing.

introduction

B*LACK IS COOL.* Let's face it, in the aggregate, black people obviously have something going for them. You take a collection of inhabitants from one cultural environment and geographic area, disparate backgrounds and worldview, and place them on the shores of a fledgling nation-to-be with a completely different cultural environment and worldview. You make *slaves* out of them. You strip from them their dignity, cultural and personal identity, and, under pain of torture and death, force them to work for mere subsistence. And what happens? A few centuries later, some of their number are among the most prominent and successful people on the planet, and one is elected as the leader of the nation where their ancestors were so unceremoniously deposited.

Just think about it: The Africans who were brought to this continent by force during the period of the transatlantic slave trade were from significantly varied tribal backgrounds. Many had little in common save for the color of their skin. Their tribal makeup included dozens of groups, including the Akan, BaKongo, Chamba, Gbe, Igbo, Makua, Mandé, Mbundu, Wolof and Yoruba. While most came from West Africa, they hailed from places as geographically diverse as Angola,

Benin, Cameroon, Cote d'Ivoire, the Congo, Gambia, Ghana, Guinea, Mozambique, Nigeria, Senegal, and Togo. Some of these groups were as culturally dissimilar as Eskimos are from Sicilians.

They thrived, however, considering the circumstances, giving rise to a rich, novel subculture, as it were. Over time, they even adopted Christianity, the faith of those who had enslaved them. For reasons that are quite open to dispute, this actually developed into something that was (and occasionally remains) more genuine than that being practiced by certain whites.

Though some argue otherwise, blacks have been very successful in America. What accounts for this success, leaving aside the innate individual and cultural strengths possessed by any individual or ethnic group?

I submit that "success," such as it is gauged by modern Americans, is largely determined by individual traits. On a more collective level, the success of blacks in America can be traced to three things.

One was the United States' cultural maturation. During the era of the American Revolution, there were men among the Founding Fathers who took issue with the fact that their stated creed conveniently and hypocritically excluded the black man. What credibility, they asked, would the words "We hold these truths to be self-evident, that all men are created equal, that they are endowed by their Creator with certain unalienable Rights" have internationally and for posterity when America had a slave class? As we know, issues of investiture won out, and the matter was put on the back burner for almost another century.

Though there were reasons other than the issue of slavery that brought about the Civil War, and reasons other than humanitarianism for the abolition of slavery, post-Enlightenment Americans had begun to examine the institution and its lack of compatibility with their stated principles, those of Christianity in particular.

With the advent of the Civil Rights Movement, not only had blacks decided, as it were, that they no longer wished to live as second-class citizens, but the white majority had undergone a considerable change of heart and mind as well. The idea that a modern society—which thought a great deal of itself—would continue to support a system wherein an entire class of people were routinely denied their basic rights as prescribed by law came to be regarded as profoundly backward.

The struggle of those blacks who endured the protests, riots, heckling, beatings, jail, and even death cannot be minimized; however, the belief on the part of white Americans that blacks ought finally to have their due cannot be denied. According to the United States Census for 1960, the total population of our nation was approximately 180 million people. Of this, 159 million were classified as "White," and 19 million as "Negro."

As this author has asserted many times, *If "whitey" had really wanted to "get" us, we'd be "got."*

While one could fill many books with causes for the Abolition Movement, the dismantling of the slave state, and finally the Civil Rights Movement, as with scores of monumental historical events, for our purposes I will distill the nature of the change down to this:

It was time.

Another reason for the success of blacks in America was the determination of individuals within the black community toward procuring those liberties that were legally guaranteed, but had been denied them since the inception of the United States. This, of course, differs from the aforementioned drive of blacks toward individual success.

The Civil Rights Movement, as such, is considered by historians to have been more of a global movement than simply one in which American minorities, and to some extent women, sought parity under the laws of the land. As education, communication, and other infrastructural areas in America improved, people who would become leaders in these movements began to see the struggles of disenfranchised people in Ireland, Africa, and other parts of the world. They learned the history of their nation and considered more deeply the hypocrisy that the Founders had contemplated two hundred years earlier. The most prominent and noteworthy was the Reverend Dr. Martin Luther King Jr.

The third factor for the success of blacks in America is something that I consider to be far less positive and righteous, although it has undeniably benefited certain black Americans in the material sense.

This is a phenomenon I call *negrophilia*. It is an undue and inordinate affinity for blacks (as opposed to antipathy toward them) that has been promoted by activists, politicians, and the establishment press for the past forty years and that has fostered an erroneous perception of blacks in the West, but particularly in America. Since the Civil Rights Movement, Americans have also been subjected to the message from the news and entertainment media, liberal politicians, and activists that people of color are somehow more noble, benevolent, and inherently less corruptible than whites.

Concurrently, the notion of whites' inherent guile, greed, and corruptibility has been promoted and reinforced. Indeed, at times it appears that most—if not all—of the world's ills have their genesis in the actions of Northern Europeans or those descended from same. "Black culture," such as is proffered in pop culture, has been vigorously promoted by the media and largely accepted by whites, particularly white youth, though it continues to have deleterious effects upon the black community at large.

Negrophilia is not by nature a *conscious* partiality toward or devotion to black people, but a subliminal persuasion toward affinity and a misconception of virtue. It is essentially the result of an ongoing propaganda campaign that has underpinned "positive" stereotypes, if you will. For example, negative stereotypes of some other ethnic groups are well known: Germans are harsh, the Polish, dumb; Jews are cheap, and the Irish are drunks. These stereotypes were the result of decades, if not centuries, of oral tradition, other ethnic groups passing racist tales from person to person, from generation to generation. Certainly, blacks have been included in this malign folklore; however, the tendency of established ethnic groups to engage in this fare was well-established long before blacks (or people other than the English) appeared in North America.

Similarly, positive stereotypes have been around for a long time as well. Negrophilia is different, however, and is a phenomenon that has not been seen before. Yes, there are overplayed positive (but equally erroneous) stereotypes that are familiar in our culture (Italians are tough, the French are great lovers), but never has a more intentional, focused, and precise mythos been developed to fortify a group that was not the majority in a society.

You can call it a conspiracy if you like; though it is conspiratorial, I don't know that I'd call it a conspiracy per se. Not all of its proponents possessed malicious intent in promoting the policies that developed out of negrophilia. Many had all the best intentions, if immature and naïve; others most definitely sought to keep black Americans in thrall while appearing to encourage their material and social prosperity.

In the intellectual sense, negrophilia is condescension; it promotes the idea that blacks cannot excel on their own merits. Negrophilia is immoral; within the parental paradigm in which our government likes to operate, negrophilia is akin to the parent who coddles the child who then experiences grave difficulty in functioning successfully when he leaves home.

Negrophilia cuts both ways as well: Black Americans have been encouraged to accept without equivocation the veracity and nobility of all black "leaders." This was not always the case; in the early days of modern civil-rights activism (that being the late nineteenth and early twentieth centuries), blacks claiming to speak for black advancement had their work cut out for them as far as gaining the trust of their would-be constituents went. Now, the latter-day compulsory allowance on the mere basis of being black has been the case for so long that critical evaluation of said leaders is no longer even considered. Whether they be activists or politicians, as long as they spout black power, entitlement, and victimization rhetoric, they are acknowledged as legitimate representatives of the black community.

When a black individual comes along who becomes prominent, there is almost total approval and deference on the part of the black community at large. To a certain extent, this was understandable forty years ago; to see anyone who was black becoming successful at anything was nearly miraculous. The problem is that this approval has been encouraged with complete absence of discernment.

There is one exception: If a successful black person is outed as leaning toward traditional values, being politically conservative, or something otherwise unacceptable by prominent blacks already on the scene, they become persona non grata. If such an individual does *not* spout the aforementioned black power, entitlement, and victimization rhetoric, well, they become something even worse than a white "oppressor."

There is also a difference in the kind and intensity of negrophilia between white and black Americans: If white Americans have been mesmerized by the phenomenon, blacks are positively spellbound. The relative number of blacks who have succumbed to this school of thought and have any hope of being "deprogrammed" is tiny. Like ideologically infused devotees of the far left (black or otherwise), they cling to these ideas and the self-appointed black leadership as if they were family. They are the ones who will most quickly and vociferously attack blacks who question negrophiliac dogma or black leaders, equating any discernment or collective introspection as a threat tantamount to reconsidering the implementation of Jim Crow.

Capitalizing on the collective guilt and shame of whites, and later, by reinforcing concepts of so-called political correctness, negrophilia has, directly and indirectly, led to a situation in which blacks—ironically, despite positive aspects of the mythos itself—are seldom held accountable for their actions or state of affairs. Predatory, opportunistic members of the black community, as well as white politicians, have used this to enrich themselves and secure political power. In the case of blacks of this sort, their intentions and their actions have been considered above suspicion. Why? Largely because the parties offering this bill of goods have always been very judicious as regards attacking with the utmost alacrity those who would raise suspicion. Essentially, anyone in society—politicians and the press, in particular—who claimed to engage in any activity or policy calculated to improve the lot of blacks in America was given a free hand.

Those free hands, holding the broadest of brushes, also erected the "virtual temple" of negrophilia.

෴

Suppose the white majority had not been willing to relinquish their social preeminence in 1964, when the Civil Rights Act was being considered by Congress? Suppose the prevailing tone in America had been one in which such legislation would never have been conceptualized, let alone considered and, finally, passed? In all likelihood, segregation and Jim Crow laws would have remained in place until such a time at which the white majority *was* of a mind to consider them in the light of morality. As mentioned earlier, whites were a resounding majority in the early 1960s—and remain so to this day. Obviously, whites believed that *it was time* too.

Yet, many blacks still stridently argue that ours is a racist nation.

Why? The answer: negrophilia. Two aspects of negrophilia are the aforementioned lack of accountability on the part of blacks, and the ingrained fear on the part of whites to call the ridiculous what it is. Set aside the election of Barack Obama as president of the United States in November 2008: It still became patent silliness to view America as a racist nation long ago. One can't swing a dead cat on television or in films without hitting a young black multimillionaire, and often they are as eager to voice the same opinion as the uneducated slumdweller who has been even more steeped in ignorance and the cult of victimization maintained by those who have made negrophilia an institution.

From "Disney Accused of Racial Insensitivity Over First Animated Black Princess," *Times of London*, April 25, 2009:

> *Even though there is a real-life black man in the highest office in the land with a black wife, Disney obviously doesn't think a black man is worthy of the title of prince.*
> —A BLACK BLOGGER

This is but one of the many thousands of examples of the effect of negrophilia put forth in the press on a regular basis. These range from passing remarks such as the one above, often mirrored by so-called black leaders, to those who keep the discussion of reparations for slavery alive in the press for weeks at a time. In the above example, Disney was excoriated for the manner in which they handled the portrayal of characters in their first full-length animated film featuring a black female protagonist. As usual, and as has been intimated (if not directly stated) many times, *nothing* will ever be "good enough" (to recompense blacks for their past inequitable treatment) in the estimation of some black Americans. If the reason for this is not clear, it will definitely become so.

To put it bluntly, black people have become lemming-like, whining crybabies, blindly following rapacious, self-seeking activists, and looking for Klansmen behind every bush. In a sense, it's not their fault; if they have been victimized, they have been victimized in the same way all Americans have been over the last forty years. Between the far-left influence in our schools and the wholesale propaganda in the press and entertainment media, those Americans capable of utilizing critical thinking skills, at this juncture, are few and far between indeed.

For my part, I am a black American, though I am actually of mixed race. I am the product of one black parent and one white one. I have always been identified as black, though I was raised to be as color-blind as possible in a society that (ostensibly) speaks to encouraging color-blindness.

The concept of "color-blindness," as America has tried to practice it, has always piqued my intellectual curiosity. I grew up in metropolitan New York during the Civil Rights Movement in the same neighborhood as Betty Shabazz, Malcolm X's widow, and their children; my mother was a teacher of African and Afro-Cuban dance, so I was keenly aware of what is commonly referred to as "black culture," perhaps more than most because there was the added emphasis on history as well as the African and black Caribbean aspects of my heritage.

One of the observations I've made on numerous occasions in my sociopolitical columns is that most of the black families I knew possessed stability, this despite the injustices of the day. Blacks owned businesses and rental properties, and were retiring with money in the bank. Almost overnight, it seemed, the children and grandchildren of these folks began dropping out of school, doing hard drugs, and having wanton sex and the resulting illegitimate offspring. Welfare rolls exploded. As strides were being made in social consciousness, civil rights, and socioeconomic parity, young blacks were self-destructing.

As the years went by, many of these (and their children) remained poor, hopeless, and embittered.

While the phenomenon is puzzling on its face, the reason for it is simple—and the reason for negrophilia as well: White progressives and black activists, many of them dedicated Marxists (as I later learned), working through fervent activism and the press, convinced these young blacks that their lot was indeed hopeless. "Whitey" was never going to let them have anything of value in life, so why try? Much of the poverty in the black community, the out-of-wedlock birth rate, and explosion of gang activity has its roots in this "movement," more aptly labeled a "cult of victimization." It should be noted here that the poverty and oft-bemoaned incarceration rates (which we'll get into presently) rose during this period.

When prominent white would-be reformers decry these conditions, they are labeled as racists. When prominent black would-be reformers do so, they are called race traitors, puppets of the white establishment, and even less flattering fare. Those who do the name-calling are the same parties responsible for the perceptions described in this book. Professional civil-rights activists, both black and otherwise, far-left politicians, and the entertainment industry and establishment press have fostered wretchedness within the black community in America while promoting perceptions of blacks that are as inaccurate, bizarre, and ignorant as some of those held by many whites prior to desegregation and the Civil Rights Movement.

ne·gro·phi·li·a

ONE

a racist nation?

*Racism: 1: a belief that race is the primary determinant of human
traits and capacities and that racial differences produce an inherent
superiority of a particular race. 2: racial prejudice or discrimination.*
—MERRIAM-WEBSTER DICTIONARY

ON NOVEMBER 4, 2008, Americans elected Barack Hussein
Obama as the forty-fourth president of the United States.
Since he was a black man, this was heralded as a monumentally historic event—the first black president in a country that was segregated
a scant fifty years ago. A historic event, yes, whether or not one sub-
scribes to theories of underhanded race politics, the evils of affirmative action, and the cult of victimization in which many hold that
black people still live.

Yet, many were distressed by Obama's election. The Democrat,
who had no executive experience, served only two years as a U.S. senator—and spent most of that time running for president.

He ran against a seasoned senator in John McCain, a Vietnam War
veteran and former prisoner of war. Little was known about Obama
and his likely policies despite two published memoirs; though he
campaigned as a centrist, his political history evidenced the most far-
left liberal tendencies.

. . .

TRINITY UNITED CHURCH AND REV. JEREMIAH WRIGHT

During the campaign, several issues surfaced that many argued ought to have sunk the candidate. Among them was that concerning the church Obama had attended for twenty years prior to announcing his candidacy, and its pastor. Upon investigation, Trinity United Church of Christ appeared to worship things African to a far greater degree than they did Christ, and gave the impression of being a separatist "church" in the same vein as do certain supremacist "white brethren" churches—or even Louis Farrakhan's Nation of Islam.

From the Trinity United Church of Christ (www.tucc.org) Web site:

> We are a congregation which is Unashamedly Black and Unapologetically Christian . . . Our roots in the Black religious experience and tradition are deep, lasting and permanent. We are an African people, and remain "true to our native land," the mother continent, the cradle of civilization. God has superintended our pilgrimage through the days of slavery, the days of segregation, and the long night of racism. It is God who gives us the strength and courage to continuously address injustice as a people, and as a congregation. We constantly affirm our trust in God through cultural expression of a Black worship service and ministries which address the Black Community.
>
> Trinity United Church of Christ adopted the Black Value System written by the Manford Byrd Recognition Committee chaired by Vallmer Jordan in 1981. We believe in the following 12 precepts and covenantal statements. These Black Ethics must be taught and exemplified in homes, churches, nurseries and schools, wherever Blacks are gathered. They must reflect on the following concepts:

> 1. Commitment to God
> 2. Commitment to the Black Community
> 3. Commitment to the Black Family
> 4. Dedication to the Pursuit of Education
> 5. Dedication to the Pursuit of Excellence
> 6. Adherence to the Black Work Ethic

7. Commitment to Self-Discipline and Self-Respect
8. Disavowal of the Pursuit of "Middleclassness"
9. Pledge to make the fruits of all developing and acquired skills available to the Black Community
10. Pledge to Allocate Regularly, a Portion of Personal Resources for Strengthening and Supporting Black Institutions
11. Pledge allegiance to all Black leadership who espouse and embrace the Black Value System
12. Personal commitment to embracement of the Black Value System.

In my 2007 column entitled "Obamination," I asked what the reaction (on the part of the public) to a white candidate might have been had he or she belonged to a church professing a similar creed, save for the "black" above having been replaced with the word "white."

The column elicited a media frenzy that continued throughout the campaign. This intensified when several samples of video footage of the church's pastor, Rev. Jeremiah Wright, began to surface. These contained some of the most vitriolic, anti-Semitic, anti-white, and anti-American rhetoric to which the American public had been exposed. Worse, Wright was unapologetic, electing to attempt to explain his remarks "in context."

In the end, Obama saw fit to leave the church. Although he never disavowed Wright, he did renounce his comments, claiming that he had never heard anything even remotely resembling the video footage during his years in the pews at Trinity United.

As far as Obama's popularity went, however, none of it seemed to matter.

WILLIAM AYERS

I chose my friends carefully. The more politically active black students, the foreign students, the Chicanos, the Marxist professors. . . .
—BARACK OBAMA, from his book *Dreams from My Father*

At least as potentially harmful—so one would imagine—was the revelation of Obama's relationship with one William Ayers. This man is advertised as a "Distinguished Professor" at the University of Illinois at Chicago. Like many former Civil Rights Movement–era radicals who later mainstreamed themselves, Ayers, a Marxist, was a leader of the Weather Underground, essentially a domestic terrorist organization. This man participated in the bombings of New York City police headquarters in 1970, the Capitol Building in Washington in 1971, and the Pentagon in 1972. After accidentally blowing up his girlfriend, our hero slithered underground for several years.

Ayers was never successfully prosecuted due to legal technicalities. Some argue that it was in part due to sympathetic parties within the criminal justice system.

As it turns out, Ayers served on two nonprofit boards with Barack Obama, one of which was the Chicago Annenberg Challenge where they worked on "education reform" for no less than five years. Both Ayers and his wife, former Weather Underground member Bernardine Dohrn, hosted a gathering at their home in 1995, where Illinois State Senator Alice Palmer endorsed Obama as her chosen successor.

Despite Obama's stated affinity for Marxism (which never surfaced in any meaningful way during the 2008 campaign) and the fact that Ayers was a living legend in the radical community, when questioned by the press, Obama initially claimed to have barely known Ayers.

"That's not the Bill Ayers I knew," was all Obama said by way of explanation, when queried about Ayers's bombing activities.

The press did not pursue it further, and the issue went away.

LARRY SINCLAIR

In early 2007, a man named Larry Sinclair contacted the Obama camp requesting that the candidate disclose his use of crack cocaine and the sexual encounters that the two men had in 1999 when Obama was an Illinois state senator. When a member of Obama's staff informed Sinclair that Obama planned to do no such thing, Sinclair proceeded to disclose his allegations publicly. Later, Sinclair—an admittedly shady character—failed two polygraph tests wherein he was questioned regarding his claims.

While acknowledging the highly questionable credibility of Sinclair (he reportedly has a long criminal record, which includes such things as convictions for forgery, theft, and the use of several aliases), one would think that such a claim—even given the small probability of truth—would have been investigated by the press rather than ignored, but ignored they were, more or less on the say-so of Obama staffers. I'm not saying that Sinclair's allegations ought to have had more media play than Bill Clinton's pre-election "bimbo eruptions," but there's also no reason they should have gotten less.

THE TRINITY UNITED MURDERS

Members of Chicago's Trinity United Church (which Obama was still attending at the time) already had their Christmas trees up when members of the Chicago press circulated through the city, interviewing many of them as they mourned the death of Donald Young, their forty-seven-year-old choir master, who had been found shot in his South Side Chicago home on December 3, 2007.

Young, known for having a flamboyant persona, was an openly gay man.

The choir director's murder and the execution-style murders of two other gay Trinity United congregants within sixty days of each other had gays and blacks terrified over the winter of 2007–2008. They feared that a serial killer targeting either blacks, gays, or both might have hung out his shingle in Chicago.

Curiously, neither then-Senator Obama (who had already announced his candidacy for president), his surrogates, nor law enforcement had much to say regarding the circumstantial connection. Nowhere in the news reports of the killings was there any mention of Obama, the questioning of him, or any of his cohorts or staffers by Chicago police.

To suggest that Obama was somehow involved in these murders is obviously a leap. However, one would correctly surmise that if any citizen, prominent or otherwise, had been publicly accused of being a closet homosexual, then three gay men from their church were murdered in the months that followed, local law enforcement would have crawled up one of their excretive orifices with an entire crime scene unit.

As the investigation ensued in the alternative press, Rev. James David Manning seemed to take on the mission of preventing the election of Barack Obama as a holy and personal crusade. The minister, who presides over New York–based Atlah World Ministries, released a flurry of anti-Obama videos that depicted the candidate as "an emissary of the devil."

The reverend asserted that Obama was at least bisexual, if not a closet homosexual, and a former drug abuser, an unregenerate sinner who was only using the issue of faith to advance himself in the political realm.

Although former Obama associate and accuser Larry Sinclair—who precipitated Obama's short-lived "gay bimbo eruption" at the beginning of his campaign—failed a polygraph test following his assertions that he had done cocaine and had sex with Obama in 1999, it does give pause that the candidate continued to be linked with sex and drugs.

Though Obama had admitted to experimentation with drugs years before, some speculated that he was concerned that his experimentation with (or immersion in) sexually adventurous realms might not sit so well with American voters. If Rev. Manning's charges contained any truth whatever, it might lend credence to accusations that the three men murdered in Chicago were victims of a conspiracy to silence those who might bring Obama's homosexual dalliances to light.

Left-wing blogs and some YouTube posters portrayed Manning as a veritable psych-ward escapee. Others found him—though brutally frank—as one who simply possessed a certain orthodoxy regarding literal obedience to Christian doctrine. Manning did meet with Larry Sinclair, and while the latter obviously had credibility problems, the pastor said that, in general, Sinclair spoke easily and knowledgably about Obama's bisexuality and crack cocaine use.

So what do we really know? What we know is that three gay members of Trinity United Church were murdered in close temporal proximity during late 2007. It is extremely unlikely that Obama never met these men, particularly the choir director. We also know that somewhat earlier, a former Obama acquaintance claimed that he and Obama had participated in gay sex and drug use. Though it was revealed that the man was lying about something, law enforcement operatives know that polygraphs are not universally reliable and even pathological liars don't lie all the time.

The tabloids the *National Enquirer* and the *Globe* began investigating Obama's alleged homosexual adventures and drug use as early as 2006. A private investigator who works with the Chicago Police Department allegedly told the *Globe* that Donald Young was silenced because of something he knew about Obama.

As we know, despite the outlandish tales sometimes spun by these publications, quite often they are spot-on as regards celebrities. A prime example was the case of Sen. John Edwards's love child. If the tabloids know anything about Obama, however, they are clearly biding their time—as may be some others.

The point is not that Obama may or may not have been guilty of this or that. Evidently he was lying about never having heard Rev. Wright rail against whites or America, and he may be lying about some of these other things. The point is that this baggage would have killed any other candidacy than Obama's, but it didn't—in my view, *for no other reason than because he is black.*

THE BIRTH CERTIFICATE

Finally, there was the issue of Obama's inability to produce an original birth certificate confirming his status as a natural born citizen of the United States. The travel habits of his parents during that period of time, as well as anecdotal evidence, strongly suggested that he might have been born in Kenya. This aspect of the candidate's background as borne out is disturbing for three reasons:

1. Having been born anywhere other than in the United States would have made Obama ineligible to serve as president.
2. The documentation presented and the behavior of Obama and his staffers in response to the issue (such as Obama ordering his birth records sealed during a trip to Hawaii to visit with his dying grandmother) tend not only to raise more suspicion but tend to validate same.
3. Though the matter was never satisfactorily resolved, no one in a position of authority or influence ever pressed the issue.

Despite this, those who consider (or worse yet, raise) the issue of Obama's eligibility are swiftly relegated to the black-helicopter or tinfoil-hat crowd by the establishment press. In fact, the question has been so vigorously touted as utter rubbish that even some otherwise reputable journalists dismiss it as nonsense without more than a glance at Obama's reissued Hawaiian "Certificate of Live Birth."

The central question at this point: *Is this the sort of man a racist nation elects as its president?*

There were practically dozens of more "minor" untoward issues, deceptions, and evasions regarding candidate Obama during the campaign. The point is that, in the aggregate, considering the scrutiny that other presidential candidates have borne, Obama's candidacy should have been sunk in mid-2007.

As president, Obama has implemented measures on a massive scale that promise (given the historical record) to be some of the most economically crippling and liberty-stultifying ever seen in our nation's history. His record spending, insinuation of the federal government into industry, overtures to transfer key sectors of the American economy to government control, and appointment of subversive individuals to key positions in his administration, as well as a shadow government of "czars" who answer to him only, have gone unchallenged by far more Americans than one would expect. It is anyone's guess how much of his radical agenda will have become reality by the time this book is published—if this book has not been ordered burned by the Obama administration, along with hundreds of others critical of him, socialism, and the Marxist encroachment into American politics.

The president routinely disparages the prior administration—something past presidents have judiciously avoided as a matter of decorum, regardless of political and philosophical differences. This has never been criticized.

Obama possesses the rare gift of being able to speak with authority on issues about which he knows nothing. In English, there is a popular colloquial term for this. He can propose measures that are frightening to the informed among us—such as imposing new, restrictive manufacturing standards on an auto industry in imminent danger of imploding—and do so conveying the absolute certainty that they are prudent, even brilliant acts. He could be the last nail in America's coffin, constitutionally speaking, yet nearly half of America sees only a noble, well-intentioned man—and isn't it wonderful that he's black?

Well, I would submit that Obama is well aware of that which I proffer here. He knows that he may propose anything he likes; all of his measures may not succeed, but those who oppose his policies, high or low, will be slandered and accused of racism by his supporters and surrogates. As of this writing, this has already occurred on numerous occasions.

One could bemoan the aforementioned details: *You stupid sons of bitches. You just* had *to have your precious first black president. You couldn't wait until someone of substance came along; you had to pick a guy who's spent his entire adult life studying every imaginable methodology for bringing this country down. Now look what you've gotten us into . . .*

Of course, this wouldn't ameliorate any of our nation's difficulties or diminish our current peril.

Personally, I don't put that kind of emphasis on race. I don't care that Obama's black; I care that he's a Marxist and a political thug. A conscientious person who *did* put an inordinate emphasis on race might be very upset that our First Black President happens to be the antithesis of everything good and decent about America. The fact is that people who put that kind of emphasis on race are typically far-left types, and those who supported Obama *because* he is black.

After the 2008 election, eager black folks asked me what I thought Obama was going to do for black Americans now that he was in office. After a good laugh, my answer was always the same: *"About as much as he did for blacks in Chicago . . ."*

While many Obama detractors attribute his victory in 2008 to the establishment press, in the main, it was negrophilia that made it possible for a candidate with all of the aforementioned political shortcomings to become president of the United States. While no white politicians—including John McCain—were willing to clamor for full disclosure where subjects like Jeremiah Wright and Bill Ayers were concerned, even the press would not have been able to ignore the outcry that would have come from American citizens over a white candidate with similar political baggage.

Why then, has Barack Obama been given a pass, not only by his peers but by American voters?

Negrophilia. This kept nearly all of the white electorate in check, either through their misguided affinity or their misplaced guilt. Obama is above suspicion. He is what he says he is; additionally, I would wager that 90 percent of those who voted for him *still* remain unapprised of his political and philosophical liabilities. It would be disingenuous to say that negrophilia was the only reason Obama was elected, but he definitely would not have been elected if not for this factor.

There is a cult of personality that is generated around presidential candidates, regardless of personality or party. In 2008, there was also the *personal* cult of Barack Obama to consider, and it was formidable due to his innate talents as well. Obama is a great speaker. Ronald Reagan had the same gift. Obama also has an uncanny knack for saying what people want to hear; he does this even better than accomplished politicians. In that election, another advantage he had was something else that we'd never seen before: the cult of the first black nominee.

All of these criteria upon which presidents are elected are wholly emotion-based. In the general election of 2008, there were millions of Americans for whom electing our First Black President superseded all other priorities. To deny this is to reject an evident illustration of human nature. This blind determination grew directly out of negrophilia. *In fact, many whites have been so conditioned via this syndrome that they don't even believe that race was a factor in Obama's election.*

To the informed, it is obvious that the far-left leadership in America (and probably beyond) wanted Barack Obama in the White House. When considered, it turns out to be eminently practical as well as shrewd: With a black electorate that will follow a black leader in lemming fashion and a white electorate that is either enraptured or frightened of being accused of racism, who better to pilot America in this quantum leap toward socialistic hell than a black man? Although few would admit it, I'd wager the majority of Americans who voted for him held a latent conviction that somehow, the manner in which a black president would operate would be fundamentally better than would a white president. With his sense of history and justice, a black man would *never* put politics or personal aggrandizement ahead of service to the nation. He would *never* compromise our national security or our economic stability, or risk the life of one American the way a soulless white suit would.

This is one of the chief reasons why Barack Obama was groomed to run in 2008; if a black man's methods and motives are sacrosanct—due to fear of being labeled a racist for criticizing him, and the myth of black benevolence and nobility—it stands to reason that it would be far easier for said black man holding the office of president to drive home a seditious and thinly veiled anti-American agenda than a white one. This was evidenced before the first year of Obama's presidency was out; based upon his policies and appointees alone, it became apparent even to many who voted for him that his politics went even beyond socialistic: They were *communistic.* Yet millions still doggedly, and even belligerently, insisted Obama was an able leader who should continue to be supported. They were so dumbed-down and suffered from racial intimidation to such a degree that they were not even aware of the events taking place before their very eyes.

Insane? Definitely—but when I said I'd wager it was true, I meant I'd wager a lot. Why would so many otherwise intelligent, sensible people elect to follow such a perilous, foolish course?

You got it. *Negrophilia.*

Appearances to the contrary, however, this is not an anti-Obama treatise. Barack Obama's election is only an extreme example of this phenomenon. Indeed, Obama's very election is one of the strongest single arguments for there being something drastically wrong with Americans' perception of race relations and the role ethnicity plays in our culture. It is one of the strongest single arguments for the existence of negrophilia.

Is the election of the first black man to office of president of the United States a monumental historical event? Given our history, of course it is. Is it a positive thing that America (which is still predominantly white) was willing to elect a black man president? Absolutely. It is just unfortunate that the first black man elected to the office was someone of Obama's character and caliber and that Americans had become so intellectually indolent that they were not able to distinguish what was being sold to them.

This book will explain—among other things—the mechanism by which it occurred.

PROPAGANDA: KEEPING THE LIE ALIVE

An ethnic joke:

Heaven is where:
The Police are British,
The Chefs are Italian,
The Mechanics are German,
The Lovers are French,
And it's all organized by the Swiss.
Hell is where:
The Police are German,
The Chefs are British,
The Mechanics are French,
The Lovers are Swiss,
And it's all organized by the Italians.

There was a time when such fare as this would not be considered particularly racist. At this juncture, I'd wager that a random cross-section of Americans would result in at least a 50-50 split in favor of the above indeed being a decidedly unacceptable example of racism. And that's sad. When I was a kid, racist individuals could be found in any chance area of encounter; institutional racism was just as common. One pizza restaurant owner of Italian descent was one of the most wonderful guys I knew growing up. He did volunteer work and mentored kids regardless of race or socioeconomic standing. To this day, people I knew as a child share their fond memories of him. He also made great pizza.

The pizza restaurant owner a mile away, also of Italian descent, was another story. The one time I visited his establishment when he was there (I'd been there before when he wasn't there), he affected ghetto black body language and began uttering Italian racial epithets. I wanted to kill him, or set fire to his store, at the very least. I was overjoyed when, some years later, he did suffer serious burns while torching the place for the insurance money. Not only was he injured, but he served jail time as well.

But I digress. When I was a kid, race was as fair game as someone having big ears, Coke-bottle glasses, or being overweight. (Yes, I know: Most of those are off limits these days as well.) Despite this, friendships were just as substantial and just as strong as those in racially homogenous cliques. If such a group confronted an ethnically diverse one and took exception to its makeup, they'd have to be prepared to fight.

Something you'd never get a contemporary, politically correct New Yorker to admit these days is that a lot of the teasing that went on back then was rooted in stereotypes that had a basis in fact. Let's be honest: How do you think stereotypes come along in the first place? Still, many kids who engaged in what would be called racist banter today had to endure excoriation and confrontation from members of their own ethnic groups for fraternizing outside of those groups. In my view, those kids had more character than today's civil-rights activists can even conceptualize.

These days, young black multimillionaires abound on television news, talk shows, and other assorted media venues. Unfortunately, they are often there to decry institutional racism and how their nation is devoid of opportunities for minority individuals. The fact that these individuals are not called out and ridiculed on these points is a wonderful illustration of negrophilia in action.

The press conference at Rutgers University, held by the women's basketball team on April 10, 2007 was positively surreal; it was in length and tone the sort of thing you'd see after half the team had been killed in a light plane crash. C. Vivian Stringer, the women's basketball coach, opined: "We have all been physically, mentally, and emotionally spent, so hurt by the remarks that were uttered by Mr. Imus. But, you see, we also understood a long time ago that, you know what? No one can make you feel inferior unless you allow them, that we can't let other people steal our joy."

This was in response to the media firestorm that erupted after New York radio "shock jock" Don Imus referred to the young black players as "nappy-headed hos" on air while he viewed one of their games. There are two reasons Imus's remarks about the team were foolish and imprudent:

1. Assuming he was aware of the unfortunate changes in our social climate (or zeitgeist), he should have known that it wouldn't play well coming from a white man.
2. It provided fodder for opportunistic black activists and validation for those who have been indoctrinated into their culture of victimhood.

Stringer's statement was also profoundly contradictory. It immediately occurred to me by virtue of her words that *they already had let their "joy" be "stolen."*

Comedian Don Rickles, though loved by millions of all ethnic backgrounds, couldn't succeed with the comedy he used to do in the sixties and seventies, when he was at the height of his popularity. If you went to one of Rickles's stand-up shows and you caught his eye— look out. Whether it was your height, weight, hair (or lack thereof), eyes, nose, ears, clothes, companion, surmised sexual preference, or race, you were going to get picked on. The thing is that no one got offended because it was all in context; that's what Rickles's shtick was. Everyone expected the barbs—some of which could really sting. There was even a classification of comedy at the time: "ethnic humor." As long as it was in the context of entertainment, everyone laughed and stuck the joke in their own bag of ethnic jokes, the only concern being the hope that they could recall it accurately enough to bring it off passably when they told it. The same goes for Buddy Hackett, who used the same kind of acerbic humor, though his was often more risqué and invective-laced than Rickles.

Today, Mel Brooks couldn't produce his now classic (and frequently "edited for content") comedy *Blazing Saddles*. Political correctness and negrophilia have abolished such fare, turning Americans into a society of eggshell-walking, thought-policed paranoiacs.

The term "racist" has been redefined. It no longer means someone who is an avowed, unregenerate bigot, or someone who has a history of acting the part but won't admit it; these days, a slip of the tongue, one careless or insensitive remark, one questionable association and you're damned. Often the accusation of another party—as during the Salem Witch Trials—is enough; the onus is on the individual to prove that they *aren't* a racist, by whatever means the accuser or accusers deem appropriate.

During the Rutgers-Imus incident, two professional race-baiting black activists, Revs. Al Sharpton and Jesse Jackson, entered the fray, as they are wont to do when there is the potential of media "face time." *Indeed, America is still an institutionally racist nation*, they intimated, thereby justifying their own craven and avaricious existence.

A few commentators were quick to point out the hypocrisies of Jesse Jackson and Al Sharpton playing the race card. Jackson, who once referred to New York City as "hymietown," has been revealed as little more than a racketeer over the last few years. Sharpton's claim to fame (if you were living in New York when he was coming up in the world and knew what he was really about) was his attempt to frame white police officers for an assault on a teenaged black girl.

There was irony, hypocrisy, and politics at work that were not lost on the astute: The tangled web of associations relative to the corporations that keep Imus and Sharpton on the air (Sharpton also has a radio show), and Jackson in the green stuff, ultimately convicted many of these players. Large media corporations also promote gangsta rappers and other purveyors of spirit poison far more racist and misogynistic than anything that emanated from Don Imus's lips. Discussions on the air and in the blogosphere were rife with Americans who recognized this hypocrisy. Then there was the fact that Imus's words were all in context; his on-air routines and past chastisements have been the stuff of broadcast industry legend for more than thirty years.

"This has never been about Don Imus," said Al Sharpton. "This is about the use of public airwaves for bigoted, racist speech. . . . We cannot afford a precedent established that the airwaves can be used to commercialize and mainstream sexism and racism."

An ironic hypocrisy that gives rise to consideration of the "America as a racist nation" contention: Why do black Americans (and many, many whites) view men like Jackson and Sharpton, as well as dozens of other activists and politicians, as righteous, admirable individuals? Is it because of all they have done for members of the black community? Given the hours of pontification they so love to deliver, I imagine that countless Americans believe they've accomplished truly significant things, but they haven't. In fact, the only thing that they've succeeded in doing is enriching themselves. Much of it is a matter of public record, some has been questionable, and some has even resulted in investigation by government agencies.

Yet, none of that seems to matter. A television anchor reports on an instance of Jesse Jackson being investigated or engaging in corporate blackmail, and the majority of black viewers reflexively bark "racist!" at the screen.

Indeed, Jesse Jackson—the most prominent of all professional civil-rights activists—has only one real claim to fame: He was present when Martin Luther King Jr. was assassinated. I imagine King is turning in his grave over what his protégé has done with his legacy.

Again—why the allegiance?

It's because they're black. There is no other reason. And *that*, dear reader, is racism.

Again, negrophilia cuts both ways; it isn't only whites who are affected. Generally, whites know that they ought to exercise discretion—even discrimination—before they confer their trust upon another person. Blacks will unequivocally trust a black activist or politician who tickles their ears, despite the fact that most of the mundane miseries they encounter are perpetrated upon them by other blacks.

Another ironic hypocrisy: Mainstream black activists answer to white progressive power brokers whose agenda is, plain and simple, to neutralize the Constitution via the "divide and conquer" method. To this end, the majority of blacks must be kept in as ignorant and wretched a condition as can be cultivated. Sharpton's call for measures to be taken to determine what may and may not be said on the airwaves was a programmed response from a programmed individual who defers to a monolithic government solution. In a sense, Sharpton was right: The Rutgers incident wasn't about Don Imus. The deeper meaning and the most important take-away from the Rutgers incident was what the actions of the poverty pimps and the media amount to: the eradication of any speech—and ultimately any thought—that the political left finds objectionable.

It is no coincidence that black activists are the ones who bring molehill issues to the fore. Since they're black, they're unassailable even if they are blatantly hypocritical, so atremble are many whites over being branded as racists.

Negrophilia is a device of the far left, socialists, and Marxists who infiltrated (and later came to dominate) the community of civil-rights activists during the 1960s. Some will argue that the lion's share of civil-rights activists were members of the far left, Marxists, and even avowed communists. The Black Panthers, for example, and certain other organizations that came out of the movement were certainly Marxist in philosophy. Though there were, indeed, some Marxists among them, the more major and influential leaders were not.

While this was going on, members of the Democratic Party, among them former segregationists, insinuated themselves and black operatives in close proximity to influential and prominent black leaders. It was these agencies that wrought the framework for the black culture of dependency. Initially, these former Dixiecrats were concerned about the advent of black political power with desegregation and the dismantling of Jim Crow. Riding the coattails of the black community's love for FDR, and then Jack and Bobby Kennedy, they ingratiated themselves to blacks; through the prospect of power and self-aggrandizement, they bought the allegiance of much of their leadership. Political programs ostensibly designed to make restitution for the way blacks had been treated (but which, in actuality, were meant to secure votes and keep blacks in a state of dependency and ignorance) were implemented. Americans were encouraged to regard as suspect anyone who questioned the prudence of these measures. After all, who but a bigot would deny blacks their due?

Prior to the Civil Rights Movement, blacks were probably among the most socially conservative groups in America. Largely, this was due to their faith and piety. They had tightly knit communities in which their pastors exercised particularly strong leadership. This is where the interlopers (Dixiecrats and far-left operatives) struck. This machination and its tragic results will be covered in greater detail in the chapter entitled "Religion."

This twofold effort not only secured the allegiance of black leadership (and the voters who followed them) for decades to come, but went a great distance to bolstering the notion that the Democratic Party was the one concerned for the "little guy" and his struggles, the downtrodden, and the underdog, which was actually quite contradictory in respect to its comportment for the previous hundred years.

By the time the far left completely subjugated the Democratic Party, they had a neatly bundled bequest in the form of dependent minorities, blacks chief among them, and a model through which they could now attempt to enroll as much as possible of the remaining population.

Concomitant with these developments, the press and the entertainment media—which had been left-leaning for some time and was becoming markedly more so—began to gratuitously promote the myth of black superiority. Efforts in this area were intensified when blacks began to become accepted in high-profile areas such as professional sports. When they excelled, they were never considered merely outstanding; held up against white athletes, they were promoted as being *better.* Black characters in cinema and television were portrayed as more spiritually enlightened, more noble, kinder, more generous—pretty much more of everything that Americans took to be positive traits in human beings. Blacks were better friends, and—of course—far superior lovers. Conversely, whites were increasingly portrayed as lacking in all of these characteristics and often replete with their opposites. To a similar degree, other ethnic minorities enjoyed the "benefits" of this legend-building apropos the change in public perception toward them. Certainly, there isn't anything wrong with representing anyone as carrying positive traits; the problem lies in that these representations were always overblown, and to the detriment of whites.

In short, it was pure propaganda that resulted in the current surreal state of affairs where race relations in America are concerned. If America is a racist nation, at this point it is only inasmuch as the majority population has been encouraged to believe in the inherent superiority of a particular race—in this case, one other than their own.

Recently I received an e-mail from a black gentleman with a family who are considering relocating to the area in which I live, one that has what is commonly known as an "emerging minority population." He was interested in the dynamics of the situation, how successfully his family might acclimatize itself to the area, and what services were available for people of color.

Research in this area is always prudent, in my estimation, and this fellow asked intelligent, reasonable questions. I answered as sincerely and honestly as I could, given my perspective—and advised him that perspective itself would have a lot to do with how he and his family would find the area and environs.

I've lived in areas where, if one were not a member of the preeminent ethnic group, one was going to have a hard time, and trying to change it in any meaningful way would have been useless and dangerous. I've also lived in places where incidents of discrimination were common, but frowned upon by most, places where one could get help if one ran into a serious problem. I've lived in places that were accepting of all people in general, and attuned to the sensitivities and sensibilities of ethnic minorities.

Finally, I've lived in places where the latter scenario was the case, but where hypersensitivity, extrinsic political influences, and propaganda really threatened the good thing the community had going with respect to race relations. For example: Media coverage of certain high-profile, hatemongering, career black activists tends to raise its head cyclically. If you're an ethnic minority who lends credence to such people, you're not going to be happy no matter where you live. It is this mindset that has resulted in some blacks remaining dissatisfied despite all of the progress they have made and that which has been made concerning race relations in America.

Can contributing, honest, hardworking people of color find a decent standard of living, good schools, welcoming places of worship, and businesses they'll feel comfortable patronizing in most communities in America? Definitely. Will they find cities and city governments that are sensitive to their sensitivities and sensibilities? Generally speaking, yes.

Unfortunately, ethnic minorities who move to areas such as that in which I live (and in similar communities) frequently also find the aforementioned purveyors of hypersensitivity, political pressure, and propaganda enticing them into the culture of entitlement and victimization. Ironically, a lot of these are white.

I'm reminded of a story about the man who was working on a highway between two towns about fifty miles apart. One man rolls up with his rented truck, his anxious family following close behind in the sedan. He explains that his company has transferred him to the town up ahead and asks the highway worker what kind of people they'll find there.

The road worker asks him: "Well . . . what were the people like in the town you just came from?"

"Oh, they were wonderful!" the man says. "From the day we moved in, it was just such a welcoming place for the family. We're sorry to have to leave."

"Well," says the highway worker, "I think you'll find the people up ahead are a lot like them."

A couple of hours later, another man drives up and stops his rented truck, his family in the SUV behind him. He explains that they're moving to the next town as well and poses the same question to the highway worker.

The worker, rubbing sweat from his brow, asks: "Well . . . what were the people like in the town you just came from?"

"Oh, man!" the gentleman snarls. "They were the rudest, most unwelcoming bunch of rubes I've ever had the displeasure of living among. From the day we moved in, it was awful. In fact, that's why I decided to ask my boss for a transfer."

"Well," says the highway worker, "I think you'll find the people up ahead are a lot like them."

As Norman Vincent Peale said: *We tend to get what we expect.*

∽

So, is America a racist nation or not? At the risk of waxing Clintonesque, that depends on your definition of "racism." Is America racist in the sense in which the accusation might have been made prior to the Civil Rights Movement? Definitely not, despite what activists and the Congressional Black Caucus might have you believe. There is simply no comparison between the social convention, prevailing thought, and institutional principles that were in place then versus now.

Sadly, because of those who keep negrophilia a vibrant, essential component of our culture, blacks and whites (as well as blacks and other ethnic groups) share a counterfeit rapport in the collective sense. Intelligent, sincere individuals across these ethnic groups have the ability to interact and forge healthy, affirmative relationships, but as a whole, these groups hold erroneous perceptions of each other and operate with a cynical apprehension that fosters tenuous and often predatory interactions.

My paternal grandmother was an off-the-boat Norwegian who was so bigoted she thought that Danish people were subhuman. Is there racism and bigotry in America? Yes, there is—and there always will be. But the idea that America is a racist nation—institutionally racist, as it was prior to the Civil Rights Movement—is patent rubbish. This is borne out by so many changes in our society, attitudes, and opportunities for blacks and other ethnic minorities that all Americans ought to find the very suggestion insulting.

So why don't we find it insulting, and why is it that many blacks routinely make the accusation?

Negrophilia. There is a deep reluctance on the part of black people to admonish their neighbors to cease their lamentation, their incessant censure of whites, and to behave responsibly. There is abject fear on the part of whites to do the same thing, terrified that Jesse Jackson and Al Sharpton will come charging into town with the press and acolytes in tow, gunning for them. And finally, the persistence of rapacious activists and politicians (who profit from this cultural phenomenon) in promoting that very behavior.

TWO

nigga, wigga, thou

I HAD A VERY good friend in junior high and high school who had a marked affinity for all things black. He was white and came from a home with reserved, well-educated, churchgoing parents. By the time we got to high school, we weren't as close as we had been previously, but I still interacted with him a lot. The transformation was one of the most bizarre things I had ever witnessed: He had gone from being a typical unkempt, long-haired, T-shirt- and Levi's-wearing preteen to a white teenager in an urban black wrapper. He dressed like the fad-obsessed, lower-middle-class black youths at our high school. He listened to the same music. He dressed as they did—which, obviously, resulted in double takes wherever he went. He even began to speak with a ghetto drawl. Even the more reserved, independent-minded black kids shuddered or rolled their eyes when he went by.

Did he have the right to behave that way? Of course—but he was *a joke.*

In a scene in the 1989 Spike Lee film *Do the Right Thing,* in one scene, Mookie and Pino (Spike Lee and John Turturro, respectively) have a discussion about race. Mookie points out to Pino that all of his idols—sports figures, movie stars, musicians—are black. Pino doesn't want to admit it, given the legendary tension between Americans of Italian descent and blacks in New York, but Mookie has indeed ensnared him.

Fast-forward thirty-five years, and my junior high school friend wouldn't get a second look. Fast-forward twenty years, and Spike Lee's Pino wouldn't make any bones about his preferences.

Why?

I could put it all down to negrophilia, but that would be disingenuous. In the main, successful sports figures, pop stars, and movie idols have earned their fan base, regardless of race, and people *are* free to admire or emulate whom they wish.

The point is that aspects of American culture, contributed by blacks, have been overwhelmingly accepted. While I knew a white girl in grade school whose mother forbade her to watch television programs with black people in them, now, the vast majority of people don't give a second thought to whites admiring or idolizing black people.

Where negrophilia fits in here, I would say, are areas wherein whites (and non-black minorities) have followed blacks into the sewer of commercialized spirit-poison. When the Women's Movement came of age in the 1970s, one of the cultural "norms" to which women took exception was the phenomenon of promiscuous men being lauded as virile, while promiscuous women were vilified as wanton tramps and sluts. Instead of acknowledging what seems like the obvious— that promiscuity is immoral, irresponsible, and dangerous, period—a significant part of an entire generation of women became wanton tramps and sluts.

In the spirit of acceptance—and, quite often, commerce—whites, and in particular, white youth, have taken to imitating the dregs of black society, those facets that are avoided by the mainstream black populace, *and even by far-left black activists.* Indeed, we do not see Jesse Jackson's children or Barack Obama's bopping around with gold chains and their waistbands across their buttocks. They are in positions of power and private schools, respectively, while their parents extol the virtues of collective desolation to young black Americans.

When the hip-hop artist Vanilla Ice came along in 1989, he was something of a novelty, and was considered as such, even by many fans. Once again, we fast-forward twenty years and Eminem (who I won't even call an artist) is taken very seriously as a rapper. Indeed, the only difference between Eminem and his black colleagues is the color of his skin. Like his black counterparts, he glorifies violence, disrespects women, and advocates a generally unproductive and extraordinarily egocentric lifestyle.

Although I participated in a token amount of media icon worship when I was in my teens, there were a few reasons I didn't take it to an extreme. One, I had already taken it into my head that I wanted to be a professional musician. Two, I had a fairly extensive background in music as an art form (as opposed to a commercial enterprise). Three, I had parents who loved music—I mean, *really* loved music—so I was raised on a steady diet of classical, jazz, blues, Afro-Cuban, calypso, and West African music, as well as AM and FM pop and rock music. In such an environment, it was difficult to hold to a fad for too long. I started teaching myself piano when I was about six.

Growing up in the metropolitan New York area, I associated freely with different ethnic groups (actually, this is more or less unavoidable in New York). A fair number of these were impoverished black people, but more importantly, culturally impoverished black people.

Here's the difference: Lots of people are poor. Some are fortunate enough to have been exposed to values that enable them to endure their poverty with dignity and to use their God-given talents and the opportunities available in our society to render their poverty academic—meaning that they may die poor, but their children probably won't. Economically impoverished, but not necessarily culturally impoverished.

Others—and this is particularly true in large cities where entitlement programs and class envy are firmly entrenched—become drawn into the mindset that is fostered, by design, in such an environment. Within a generation or two, faith, family, belief in education, ethics, and personal responsibility become alien concepts. Culturally impoverished as well as economically impoverished.

While it is undeniable that black culture has contributed immeasurably to American art forms, like the questionable values that abound in urban areas, questionable art forms also have their genesis in these cultural tide pools.

As a child, I used to play games with other kids. During the course of play, kids sometimes sing songs and recite rhymes. Hanging out with many of these culturally impoverished black kids, occasionally I would hear (and occasionally participate in) a form of rhyming that, ironically, had its roots in jazz and Southern blues.

It was base. It was profane. It was gratuitously spiked with a degree of violence and sexual innuendo inappropriate for the age of the kids who were reciting it.

It was rap.

We're talking about five-to-ten-year-old kids, by the way. Back in, oh, around 1967. The only difference was lack of production. No synthesizers, drum machines, sampling, or loops. But it was the same thing nonetheless. Lots of black people will know what I'm talking about, though I doubt that many will admit to it.

Years later, as a semi-professional musician frustrated with the degree to which I perceived I would have to compromise my artistic integrity to avoid living in a Maytag box while working in the music industry, I made a passing—but prophetic—comment to a band mate: "Before you know it, people are going to be making millions spouting that foul-mouthed crap we used to hear out on the stoop—and we'll still be trying to get our foot in the door."

Contrary to what multiculturalists would have us believe, rap is no more a substantive or integral part of black culture than pimpery or drug addiction. Despite the fact that the entertainment industry would have us believe that this "art form" is innocuous and even valuable, the gesticulating, unhygienic illiterates who compose this refuse are being idolized and emulated by American kids. Those whose parents do not have the presence of mind to curtail their exposure to them will be lost.

Rap is garbage. It has always been garbage, one of the lowest forms of so-called art, born of a culture that recognizes urine-immersed religious icons and public sex acts with root vegetables as art.

As much of a capitalist as I am, I hate to admit that, in the end, we have to follow the money. Record company executives, entrepreneurs, and venture capitalists who favor the bottom line over the kind of world their descendants will have to live in are far more to blame than a handful of undereducated, foul-mouthed, marginally talented thugs who were born into a society that had long since abandoned its values.

On May 17, 2004, legendary black comedian Bill Cosby blasted the NAACP, the NAACP Legal Defense and Education Fund, and Howard University at the gala celebration of the fiftieth anniversary of the *Brown v. Board of Education* desegregation decision, upsetting the applecart of black activism to no mean degree when he criticized blacks for abdicating various personal and social responsibilities.

Cosby's very public censure of blacks for rebuffing the many opportunities for education and social advancement open to them earned him wide excoriation in the black and (to a slightly lesser degree) mainstream press. He was accused of being too harsh, lacking compassion, and not being able to relate either because he's too old or too rich. Generally, many black activist types felt that being dragged to the woodshed by the indisputably respected elder was completely uncalled-for and counterproductive.

Few, if any, chastised Cosby for not being "black enough" or for being an establishment puppet, since Cosby has enthusiastically supported mainstream black causes and activists such as Jesse Jackson over the years. It all would likely have been forgotten, a forgivable faux pas born of frustration on the part of the beloved entertainer.

But then he did it again.

On July 1 of that year, Cosby once more collectively spanked black people at Jesse Jackson's Rainbow/PUSH Coalition and Citizenship Education Fund Conference when he criticized blacks' skills in the areas of parenting and domestic relationships.

Again, the press—mind you, not blacks at large—got monumentally ticked. Don Babwin's Associated Press article of July 2 began, "Bill Cosby went off on another tirade against the black community Thursday . . . ." On July 3, *The Black Commentator* Web magazine ran an article that dripped vitriol with the potency of molecular acid. Obviously, the attitude on the part of the black and mainstream press was: *What is he doing? He's supposed to be one of us!*

And by "one of us," they did *not* mean a person of color.

Were Rush Limbaugh or Pat Robertson to say such things, they'd be tarred and feathered in the press for a day or two, but it would be expected of them. If Thomas Sowell or I were to do so—well, we're just Oreo neocon puppets of the white establishment. Again, expected.

But when one of them, tested and true, says such things, it's another matter entirely. I mean—in the name of all things politically correct—he even used *the N-word.*

Suddenly, Cosby became like the drunken uncle who upsets family gatherings. Sure, he's well-heeled, generous, and funny, but then he goes over his limit. Even though many of the guests appreciate his antics, he still winds up embarrassing the hell out of the host.

Much of the criticism Cosby received came from the younger black press, as well as a few profiteers such as rap producers and publishers who have a stake in rotting black minds. Typically, traditionalist whites (and Oreo neocons) are quickly accused by these people of attempting to "deprive black folk of they *cultcha*" (I cannot attribute this quote to anyone in particular, but I've heard it probably on at least as many occasions as you have). This *cultcha* is, of course, little more than a cult of mediocrity, which is the point Cosby made so well. Indeed it was, as they say in the MasterCard commercial, "priceless" to see simple common sense overtake someone of Cosby's iconic respect and influence.

Also priceless were the expressions on the faces of Jackson and other heavy-hitters present when these incidents occurred. They're a combination of the embarrassed host as he frets over the intoxicated uncle and that of the older sibling who bought the bag of pot the younger one got busted with. *Will he squeal? Will this come back to burn me?*

Because it is Jackson himself who has been instrumental in actualizing the malaise about which Cosby railed, spouting pseudo-poetic bastardized Tony Robbins aphorisms to youth audiences while supporting the socialists who have conspired to keep blacks in that very cult of mediocrity—and becoming a multimillionaire in the process.

Of course, everything Cosby said was 100 percent spot-on true, but in the end, other than concerning the sanctity of personal responsibility, blacks as individuals oughtn't be blamed for their shortcomings any more than anyone else who has bought into progressivism and allowed their families and communities to degenerate into self-seeking, undisciplined entities. It's the foremen such as Jesse Jackson, working beneath their socialist overseers in the ongoing design to debase black America, who are the real villains in this tale.

So, spurred on by rapacious and irresponsible marketers, whites have now bought into the same antisocial paradigms that are aiding in the destruction of the black community. Along with rap, white youth can now be seen bopping down streets, heard blasting rap tunes and adopting the ghetto drawl, and dressing like prison bitches. (As an aside: I find it hysterical that these kids—not just the white ones—have no idea whatsoever that the style of wearing one's waistband across one's buttocks comes straight from the penitentiary; there it marks one as another con's "bitch," or sexual property.)

And it's all acceptable. Why not? If it's acceptable for a black kid to like rock music (which, ironically, was rooted in black music forms anyway), James Bond, or hockey, it would be racist to deny white kids the same opportunity to enjoy "black" art forms, right?

Unfortunately, like the sluts of the seventies, the issue of quality and character is wholly overlooked. Consequently, whites have assumed the very worst of what "black America" has to offer. But hey, at least they're accepting . . .

THREE

setting the record straight

*I find, since reading over the foregoing Narrative that I have, in
several instances, spoken in such a tone and manner, respecting
religion, as may possibly lead those unacquainted with my religious
views to suppose me an opponent of all religion. To remove the
liability of such misapprehension, I deem it proper to append the
following brief explanation. What I have said respecting and against
religion, I mean strictly to apply to the slaveholding religion of this
land, and with no possible reference to Christianity proper; for,
between the Christianity of this land, and the Christianity of Christ,
I recognize the widest, possible difference—so wide, that to receive
the one as good, pure, and holy, is of necessity to reject the other as
bad, corrupt, and wicked. To be the friend of the one, is of necessity
to be the enemy of the other. I love the pure, peaceable, and impartial
Christianity of Christ: I therefore hate the corrupt, slaveholding,
women-whipping, cradle-plundering, partial and hypocritical
Christianity of this land. Indeed, I can see no reason, but the most
deceitful one, for calling the religion of this land Christianity. I look
upon it as the climax of all misnomers, the boldest of all frauds, and
the grossest of all libels. Never was there a clearer case of "stealing the
livery of the court of heaven to serve the devil in." I am filled with
unutterable loathing when I contemplate the religious pomp and
show, together with the horrible inconsistencies, which every where
surround me. We have men-stealers for ministers, women-whippers
for missionaries, and cradle-plunderers for church members. The
man who wields the blood-clotted cowskin during the week fills the
pulpit on Sunday, and claims to be a minister of the meek and lowly
Jesus. The man who robs me of my earnings at the end of each week*

meets me as a class-leader on Sunday morning, to show me the way
of life, and the path of salvation. He who sells my sister, for purposes
of prostitution, stands forth as the pious advocate of purity. He who
proclaims it a religious duty to read the Bible denies me the right of
learning to read the name of the God who made me.
—From *Narrative of the Life of Frederick Douglass, an American Slave*

WHILE I WAS well aware of the barbarity of slavery and the man-
ifest hypocrisy of those Americans who had owned slaves and
professed Christianity, I was nonetheless disgusted and horrified by
the accounts related in the writings of Frederick Douglass.

It may be as puzzling to the reader, as it was to me, that the descendants of those who had been brought from Africa could have embraced
the religion of those who enslaved them. Indeed, some of Douglass's
writings intimate that Christianity itself was what was "wrong" with slaveholding Americans; however, the above passage refutes this. It was the
biblical perversions to which some slaveholders adhered and the general hypocrisy among slaveholding American Christians that offended
this former slave's sensibilities—and that of many whites of his era.

As regards the black slaves who came to follow Christ, it appears
that there were at least some white Christians who were doing something right.

SLAVERY IN AMERICA

The history books—which have undergone drastic changes over the
last forty years—relate a superficial and disingenuous account of
slavery in the Americas, specifically in colonial America. The average American's edification of slavery consists of white men in long-
boats coming ashore on the African continent, then lying in wait in
the jungle with nets. These they would use to ensnare hapless tribe-
speople, whom they would spirit away to North America in the excre-
ment-filled holds of tall ships. The rest, as they say, is history. The only

variation on this would be when the slavers burst upon unsuspecting villages and kidnapped the entire lot. Most of us learned about the slavers, where they came from, the tall ships, and the horrible and often deadly conditions aboard the transatlantic slave ships.

The real story is not quite so black and white—no pun intended.

It is generally accepted by Americans of the most divergent political persuasions that America was born of a combination of idealism and greed. Some came to the North American continent to escape religious persecution, while others sought fortune and glory. It is the story of many campaigns of exploration throughout history, regardless of the period or the ethnic groups involved.

By the Middle Ages, the institution of slavery had been all but abandoned on the European continent. This was mainly due to the rise of Christianity; revolutionary political developments such as the Magna Carta further dissociated Anglo-European societies from such retrograde practices.

Slavery has, however, always been a practicable commercial concern in Africa, and still is to this day. When Portuguese explorers landed on the North African continent in the 1440s, they found slavery alive and well.[1] Slaves were typically Africans who had been ostracized from their communities for any number of reasons, captured in war (where they became de facto commodities), or had been sold into slavery outright by their chieftains. At the time, the Portuguese had a very lucrative sugar interest in islands they had acquired off the northwest African coast. When these expanded onto the continent, their involvement in the slave trade became an integral component thereof.

Later, when the Portuguese and the Spanish began incursions into (first) South America, Mexico, the Caribbean, and North America, they brought the institution of slavery with them. Over three hundred years, Brazil absorbed more African slaves than anywhere else and became, as it were, an Afro-American territory.[2]

The Portuguese and the Spanish made vast fortunes during this time in sugar and mining silver in the Americas, long before any of the Northern Europeans began their expansion into the region in a meaningful way. This is certainly not to minimize the extent of the involvement of Northern Europeans in the slave trade, but it must be appreciated that the institution was well-established as a commercial enterprise and a component of the economy in the Americas when Northern Europeans arrived. The first Africans were brought to a Jamestown tobacco plantation as indentured servants in 1619. It bears mention that whites were also readily utilized as indentured servants in the Americas. Black chattel slaves began arriving in North America in the 1700s.

As mentioned earlier, the issue of slavery was a contentious one as the colonies entered into the Revolutionary War era, but the institution endured. By the 1800s, black slaves accounted for a gigantic servile class, particularly in the South. Contrary to popular belief (or propaganda), slavery did not extend to the Northern states as a widespread practice due to reasons of agricultural viability and commercial factors, rather than the righteousness of Northerners.

Another fact that is always conveniently overlooked by activists, certain politicians, the press, and revisionist historians is the fact that all free people were allowed to own slaves in the colonies, and subsequently in the new United States; many said personages of sufficient means did in fact own slaves. This included free blacks and Native Americans. The fact that these nonwhites engaged in reprehensible practices does not, of course, excuse the whites who did so. However, it flies in the face of the popular racist American notion that suggests—and has many Americans believing—that whites are the only race ever to have enslaved another. This perception has to be eradicated from the collective mind of America if we are to have anything resembling healthy relations between ethnic groups in the United States.

The annals of American history are replete with the internal conflict given rise by slavery and opposition to slavery, both before and after the Civil War. Legislation, disputes concerning what was acceptable concerning slaves' rights when transporting them across territorial (and later state) lines, and legal obligations as regards escaped slaves who managed to make it to free territories (or states) all contributed to the conflict that erupted in 1861. In any event, the Thirteenth Amendment to the Constitution officially ended slavery in 1865.

The aspect of negrophilia that demonizes whites, along with the necessity of the far left to subvert Americans' view of our country, has given rise to a campaign that over the last forty years has portrayed America's Founding Fathers in a decidedly unflattering light. After all, many of them were slave owners; under these men, who drafted our Constitution, blacks were only considered to be three-fifths of a human being. These points of fact have, of course, gained a great deal of traction over the years regarding their usefulness as anti-American propaganda. In addition to the worldview of these "old, dead white guys" being out-of-touch with modern America, it gives rise to the question of whether the entire system they constructed might be unsound as well as outmoded. The lack of education American schoolchildren have received over this period of time in the area of history and civics has (by design) added to the proliferation of ignorance in this area as to the founders of this nation, who they were, and their worldview.

Those who have actually studied the Age of Enlightenment, as it pertains to colonial America and the Revolutionary War, are aware that (as mentioned earlier) many of the framers of the Constitution knew that the issue of slavery was a hypocrisy and would come back, like a curse, to plague the nation, if indeed we became a nation with the institution of slavery still in place. Though economics won out, the founders knew that, had slaveholders in the South been able to count their slaves as "whole people," Southerners could have overturned every effort to eliminate slavery by virtue of their population.

Hence, the "three-fifths" rule. It was not a racist pronouncement that blacks were inferior; it was a political maneuver, and a noble one.

Then there is the phenomenon of modern Americans assessing slavery from our twenty-first-century standpoint. This is unwise, though it is precisely what social engineers in our government want us to do. Cultural maturity and moral development must be considered.

During the time of the Old Testament, polygamy and women as chattels were acceptable, as was slavery. In the first democratic, post-Renaissance societies, one had to hold land in order to be able to vote. Then, it was only the men who had the privilege. The movements that changed all of these, including abolitionism and the Civil Rights Movement of the 1960s, were, in part, the results of emerging social and moral consciousness. Some came about with the advent of Christianity, some, with the dawn of the Enlightenment. Why they came when they did hardly matters; the point is that judging the actions of historical figures based on modern sensibilities is not a particularly intelligent exercise.

I would remind the reader here—as an observation, not a justification—that there are still societies in which certain (if not many) of these institutions are still considered acceptable. If we're going to condemn our system of government based on the ideas and actions of the men who implemented it, then we ought definitely to condemn that which the socialist elites among us wish to implement. The latter has given rise to far more grievous social injustice than George Washington and Thomas Jefferson ever did. There is no reason why black Americans, despite past discrimination, should not view our system of government and our society at large as providing more opportunity for them than any other in history.

But no, they see their Congressional Black Caucus—all far-left Democrats—embracing the leaders and political model of places like Cuba and Venezuela. Motivated by power—or sheer stupidity—they feed American blacks the unmitigated lie that socialism is somehow superior to a republic and that blacks will get on far better in such a system.

In April of 2009, the Congressional Black Caucus traveled to Cuba. The trip was ostensibly an overture toward improving U.S. relations with that country. It was not a maiden voyage, but it was the first time the group had traveled to the island nation since its dictator, Fidel Castro, fell ill in 2006. He was subsequently replaced by his brother Raul (who is every bit the brutal, ruthless communist as Fidel), but remains very involved in Cuba's government.

On its face, one might wonder why a group of congressional representatives would engage in such folly in the first place, but the Congressional Black Caucus has a history of embracing anything and everything that is socialistic, communistic, Afrocentric (read "racist"), and America-phobic. While some are likely brainwashed unfortunates (they often come off as quite dull), others are vintage, hardened radicals who would indeed sooner see a government such as that in Cuba replace ours.

Like Illinois Rep. Bobby Rush, for example (no relation to yours truly, I assure you). Like many black activists, Rush possesses credentials that appear quite impressive at first blush, but prove to be window dressing, a façade that masks a caustic and subversive agenda. Case in point: He was a cofounder of the Illinois Black Panther Party, a sixties-rooted group of murderous, communist thugs who sought to take over America by the gun. While this ought to have exempted him from public service altogether, obviously it has played very well.

It was almost like listening to an old friend.
—REP. BOBBY RUSH, on the Congressional Black Caucus's
meeting with Fidel Castro

The comportment of the Congressional Black Caucus members at a press conference that followed their return, with their belligerent black nationalistic edge and the abject treason underlying their effort, was overlooked because they're black—an example of negrophilia at work—and because we have a like-minded majority contingent in the establishment press.

The Congressional Black Caucus and the far left (most notably, certain dolts in the entertainment industry) would have us believe that the treatment of blacks in Marxist "paradises" such as Cuba is far superior to that which they "suffer" here in America. They fail to mention—or refuse to recognize—the fact that there aren't any blacks in positions of power in the Castro government; there never have been. The idea that Cuba—or any communist nation—has proven a haven for blacks is pure, propagandistic pap. Examine the standards of living or the general lot of people in African communist nations if you doubt.

REPARATIONS FOR SLAVERY

One of the most poignant examples of negrophilia in action, this doctrine, if you will, states that black Americans should be somehow compensated for slavery. In June of 2009, the U.S. Senate issued a formal apology to black Americans for slavery and the "Jim Crow" laws that were in force from 1876 to 1965; these were the laws that imposed segregation in the United States In July of 2008, the House of Representatives had passed a similar measure.

Although this issue has been on the drawing board for years, I knew that reparations for slavery would become an issue were Barack Obama elected president, though I harbored doubts that he would tie himself to initiating the debate directly. Interestingly, the president's proclivity for introducing measures through surrogates in Congress (which, to be fair, is a common device for presidents) became apparent within days of his inauguration. A few months into his presidency, it then became apparent that the elite left was laying the groundwork for (at least) a discussion of reparations. Although much of this was initially under the radar, there were certain signs that this was afoot, if one knew where to look.

Although the aforementioned elite left has what they consider to be very cogent, legalistic reasons and precedents for reparations, the reasoning for same is right out of an episode of *The Twilight Zone:* "In this week's episode in an exotic venue, Character A is cited for jaywalking. At the arraignment, we learn that his penalty, if he is convicted, will be death . . ."

It has been demonstrated repeatedly over the years that the sanctity of personal responsibility and accountability are on the far left's hit list. No one is responsible for anything; this has led to various forms of havoc, whether it be in politics or the criminal justice system. As such, there is no ethical deterrent toward holding one group of people responsible for the actions of another group. In this case, Americans at large will be compelled to pay black Americans for the transgressions of those long-dead Americans who enslaved their long-dead ancestors. It is my personal view that those who advocate reparations for slavery possess a degree of iniquity and malevolence so extreme that I am reluctant to disclose what I think their disposition ought to be.

The rational arguments against reparations are quite stark. Notions of justice, integrity, and equity—not to mention common sense—dictate that penalizing twenty-first-century Americans for the actions of their seventeenth-through-nineteenth-century ancestors is not only unjust, but quite insane. Additionally, working from within the same paradigm, there is no rational argument for modern black Americans somehow being deserving of recompense for the iniquities perpetrated upon their ancestors.

If this moral obscenity becomes reality, it will be negrophilia, coupled with a healthy dollop of greed, that brings it to pass.

To those Americans who can see beyond emotion and propaganda, it is obvious that our despicably vile, depraved, and avaricious lawmakers view reparations as another gargantuan wad of cash for them to administer. Then, having executed this hustle, there are the votes they perceive they will secure in perpetuity from blacks.

As they have done concerning all Americans, socialist lawmakers are appealing to the baser nature of blacks: sloth, greed, anger, and a sense of entitlement. Who, having been utterly propagandized, brainwashed, and undereducated by the government, would refuse a check from that government? It is a frightening prospect, but here the prudent gambler would put his money on nearly every black American who voted for Barack Obama climbing aboard Reparations Rail Lines as soon as an opportunity presents itself. Guilty-feeling white fools, given yet another chance to feel magnanimous with respect to their role in "healing" between the races, will promote this sham, possibly with more gusto than their black neighbors.

[FOUR]

the civil rights era—
and beyond

Lest I be taken as an apologist for slavery and the exploitation of blacks in America, the institutional management by whites of those of predominantly African heritage was, until the middle of the twentieth century, barbarous, hypocritical, cruel, shortsighted, avaricious, cavalier, arrogant, and careless—in short, evil. As a Christian, I must say that from a Christian perspective it was nothing short of an abomination.

In a sense, one could convincingly argue that between "guilty" whites and those whites on the far left, white Americans have generally exacerbated the effects of past mistakes and injustices.

The crucial point is that those with political agendas made certain that those injustices became and remained more than unpleasant footnotes in American history; when one studies the overview to which the average American is exposed from school age onward, one would think that no race had ever been exploited until blacks were brought to the Americas, and that Northern Europeans were the only ethnic group ever to have engaged in such horrid fare.

The American Civil Rights Movement, or "The Southern Freedom Movement" as it was once widely called, is generally considered to have begun in 1954 with the landmark Supreme Court decision *Brown v. Board of Education*. There isn't a great deal that can be said about the history of the Civil Rights Movement with which most educated Americans are not acquainted. Events occurred. The status quo changed. What *can* be said (that is relevant to our little excursion here) pertains to the social dynamic at the time and collective perception of the process.

The sins of the fathers were, with the abolition of slavery, essentially visited upon those who had enjoyed generations of the cheapest labor around. Given the era during which slavery flourished, and the need to keep those enslaved in a state of perpetual wretchedness, no doubt it was almost natural for a cult of black inferiority to emerge. The (white) society that had convinced itself for so long (through the necessity of their rationalization) that blacks were only slightly more advanced than apes suddenly perceived the cage door ordered open by an outside agency that cared little whether or not they were devoured by the beasts within.

Since Europeans had kept the specter of slavery from their shores (despite profiting handsomely from it), the American versus the European perceptions of blacks went down two entirely different roads.

Whites—predominantly, but not exclusively in the South—were faced with a population of blacks who, while not yet equal, also presented a real potential for competition in many areas. Black colleges began to spring up in earnest. Black entrepreneurs and landowners who had been freed prior to the Civil War were now at liberty to expand their fortunes on a greater scale and in a more overt manner.

Socially, of course, this fear of competition among whites—particularly less-educated, poorer whites—gave rise to the well-remembered cult of bigotry. This played to the basest and most irrational fears and apprehension whites had. Blacks might breed whites into nonexistence. They might come to own everything. Charging through the streets of the South (perhaps on elephants, like Hannibal), black men would pluck white women from their beds and spirit them away to be profaned. Here the irony (as well as relevance) is that these disgusting examples of bigotry are the very stereotypes that would be turned on their ears with the advent of negrophilia.

Thus, the Ku Klux Klan was born. In 1865, veterans of the Confederate Army formed the Klan, primarily to resist the efforts of Reconstruction. This they accomplished through the beating, killing, and general intimidation of freed blacks and white Republicans, the latter of whom were viewed as abolitionists and traitors to their race. As Klan chapters multiplied, other "subversive" elements such as Jews and Catholics often made Klan hit lists. The Klan's membership came to include men from the working class to lawmakers in Washington, and its influence continued fairly much unabated until the Civil Rights Movement.

The States' Rights Democratic Party (commonly known as the Dixiecrats) was a segregationist splinter group of the Democratic Party that formed in 1948. This was comprised of politicians who did not favor the gravitation of the party toward civil justice for black Americans. While the party didn't survive, the Dixiecrats didn't go away. Some returned to the Democratic Party, while some of that persuasion had never left. This is important because it is the politicians of this stripe who would help to formulate the entitlement culture in which post–Civil Rights Movement blacks would live. Through entitlements, the Dixiecrats sought control over blacks; while bigoted, most still believed in the republic and capitalism. The left-leaners simply sought conquest; ingratiating themselves to blacks was just an objective toward that goal.

Though the far left, which by the 1960s was beginning to make inroads into the Democratic Party, also favored entitlement programs, their agenda differed from the Dixiecrats in that they were a mix of soft socialists, envisioning an America that more resembled (what was at the time) Western Europe. The other contingent was made up of Marxists who sought to insinuate communist ideals into the American mainstream.

I have never been one to make the blanket accusation that white Southerners were inherently more bigoted than whites in the North, but it is undeniable that the large-scale confrontations (concerning race and race relations in the 1860s and one hundred years later) had their genesis in the South. Some might offer convincing arguments that the problem of white bigotry was more prevalent in the South. Since I was raised in the North and happen to be black, I will reserve judgment on this point. Suffice it to say that the global implications of the policies and dynamics involved are more germane to this topic than my personal opinion, particularly since I have no frame of reference.

It was a "perfect storm" series of events that ingratiated the Democratic Party to black Americans. In June of 1963, Alabama Governor George Wallace barricaded the entrance of the University of Alabama to Vivian Malone and James Hood, two black students who wished to enroll. President John F. Kennedy intervened by sending in federal marshals and the Alabama National Guard. Bobby Kennedy, the U.S. attorney general at the time, had a similar commitment to civil-rights causes.

John F. Kennedy's address delivered June 11, 1963, referenced this incident and made a pointed statement as to his administration's stance on civil rights.

I hope that every American, regardless of where he lives,
will stop and examine his conscience about this and other related
incidents. This Nation was founded by men of many nations and
backgrounds. It was founded on the principle that all men are created
equal, and that the rights of every man are diminished when
the rights of one man are threatened.
—JOHN F. KENNEDY, June 11, 1963

His speech that night laid the framework for what would become the Civil Rights Act of 1964. Though JFK's party disfavored the act, and it would not be passed until after his death, it was passed under a Democratic president. From that moment forward, Democratic politicians were given authority—or so it appeared—over civil-rights issues. Why the Democratic Party took advantage of this opportunity to put blacks in its pocket is fairly evident: Political parties live and die on the power of voters and lobbyists. Additionally, it was a chance to counterbalance one hundred years of bad public relations—which they obviously pulled off very successfully. How Democrats mustered the impudence to do so is unknown; why Republicans—who actually supported the Civil Rights Act—did not move to edify the black community as to their backing of the legislation and what the Democrats' true motives were, remains a mystery.

In the late 1960s, the red, black, and green Pan-African flag began to be used as a universal symbol of black solidarity in America. Originally designed in 1920 by the Universal Negro Improvement Association and African Communities League, the "black liberation flag" began to appear on posters, patches, in artwork, and on clothing. The flag bore resemblance to the flags of various West African nations (such as Ghana) and was widely used by militant groups and to signify militancy in general. To astute Americans who were around during this era, it was evident that at least some recognized the profitability of black activism and militancy. More of these profit-conscious Americans, both black and white, would follow.

While it would be remiss to address the civil-rights era without mention of the real pioneers and heroes thereof, suffice it to say that our educators and media—given their objectives—have done a stellar job of informing Americans as to who they were. Again, it is the underlying dynamic of the movement and contributions of these people that are being examined here.

We know that Rev. Dr. Martin Luther King Jr. accomplished great things despite certain personal shortcomings. What untold numbers of Americans don't know is that he's probably turning in his grave over what has been done to blacks in the last forty years. Dr. King has become so iconic that few Americans actually listen to his speeches or read his writings; they are also not encouraged to. If they did, they might see the inconsistencies between what he strove for and where those who picked up his mantle have taken black people.

∽

While Malcolm X (El-Hajj Malik El-Shabazz, born Malcolm Little, in 1925), the national spokesman for the Nation of Islam from 1952 to 1964, leaned toward separatism and militancy for a great deal of his career, what is seldom spoken about is the change in his worldview after his pilgrimage to Mecca. Most Americans (particularly black Americans) are familiar with catchphrases such as "by any means necessary," but are unfamiliar with the reasons he left the Nation of Islam (which are the same reasons the organization is viewed by many as a dangerous cult to this day). Elijah Muhammad, the Nation of Islam's supreme leader, was little more than a racketeer, and Malcolm discovered this. While adherents like Malcolm and others were interested in spiritual truths and ending black oppression, Muhammad was a proto–career–activist, primarily concerned with his own fiefdom and libidinous indulgences. It is widely believed—even by Malcolm's own children—that Louis Farrakhan, the exalted leader of the Nation of Islam today, orchestrated Malcolm's assassination.

∽

Millions of Americans—many whites included—believe that the Black Panther Party, while confrontational, was an honorable and virtuous society dedicated to desegregation and the advancement of black people. The party was founded in 1966 in Oakland, California by Bobby Seale and Huey P. Newton. Ostensibly, it was a community organization that was concerned with protecting blacks from police brutality (California has had a reputation for police brutality for almost a century, and not just restricted to blacks) and aiding impoverished blacks. Whether its leaders were communists from the beginning or evolved into same is difficult to discern, but the organization did become increasingly Marxist-leaning as time went on.

The Black Panthers' platform oscillated wildly between Marxism and garden variety socialism during its existence. Indeed, it is a matter of public record that their leaders had been inspired by communist icons such as China's Mao Zedong. They are best known by many Americans for their confrontations with the legal system. Being an openly militant, gun-toting outfit, they were constantly under the eye of law enforcement, including the Federal Bureau of Investigation. Gun battles between the Panthers and police, murders in which the Panthers were involved, and the high-profile trials of members Huey

Newton and Angela Davis, made for stimulating media fare during the sixties and early seventies. Between the efforts of law enforcement, their self-destructive tendencies, and the fact that most blacks were more interested in mainstreaming than overthrowing the country, the Panthers fizzled out in the early seventies. Founder Huey Newton was shot to death in Oakland during a botched drug transaction in 1989.

✍

The NAACP (National Association for the Advancement of Colored People) by its name gives one an idea of how long it has been around. Its story is one of the most unfortunate in the realm of civil-rights activism. This organization is, of course, one of the most prominent advocates for black people (at least ostensibly) in America. Founded in 1909 by W. E. B. Du Bois and just over two dozen black and white scholars, when the NAACP came into being, Jim Crow was still the law of the land in many states, particularly in the South. Additionally, the federal government not only condoned laws that preserved segregation, but actually supported them in most instances.

Utilizing the courts and growing public sympathy, Du Bois and his colleagues sought to end segregation, plainly put. They were involved in dozens of landmark legal battles, including *Brown v. Board of Education.* Unfortunately, during the 1960s and 1970s, the organization went the way of many other blacks and Northeastern intellectuals during the Civil Rights Era; they began to gravitate toward the political left. Their leadership began to consist of those who sought to make a career out of activism rather than those who were concerned, accomplished members of the community. They supported the Democratic Party's curriculum of entitlements as restitution, and became beholden to that party, more or less in perpetuity.

One of the nation's earlier civil-rights pioneers, Booker T. Washington (1856–1915), was a hero to blacks when I was growing up. An educator, speaker, and author, Washington was the first and the last, as far as civil-rights issues for black Americans went, in his day. In 1881, Washington founded the renowned Tuskegee Institute in

Alabama. His significance has been downplayed in recent years, largely because of the NAACP's increased inclination toward functioning *ad modum* the political left. Washington, who was active during the late nineteenth and early twentieth centuries, understood the fear of many whites pertaining to the emergence of black political power, how potentially dangerous it was, and sought to assuage it. Inasmuch as whites realistically held the fate of blacks in their hands, and the Ku Klux Klan had established its political clout, Washington saw fit to address whites' fears and appeal to them on a level more akin to that which Dr. King would a half century later. His message was more one of brotherhood than of stipulation. As such, he was viewed as not being "militant enough" by W. E. B. Du Bois. This view apparently matured with the NAACP's gravitation to the left.

Although the NAACP lost some of its influence after the Civil Rights Movement, it enjoyed a resurgence in the 1990s, but by then was a wholly different organization from the one which had struggled through the first half of the century. Personal aggrandizement of its leaders and unremitting, reflexive cries of victimization made it irrelevant to politically aware Americans.

Though financial troubles, questions regarding their accounting, and a few controversial leaders tainted their image, by 2000 the NAACP had become so well-established as an American icon that it retained respectable political influence, a financial base, and dedicated donors. Its message and mission, like that of most black activist organizations, has become one of paranoia and black entitlement rather than black progress. It simply toes the line for the progressive-socialist apparatus. A college scholarship fund here and a free clinic or two there don't count for much when the organization stalwartly supports the political machine that keeps millions of blacks poor, ignorant, resentful, and hopeless. It is safe to say, albeit sadly, that this can be applied to quite a few organizations and nouveau-riche black philanthropists.

౷

Unfortunately, in nominating and getting elected the first black president of the United States, the Democratic Party has probably cemented its legacy for all time as the sole champion of black people. Having so effectively wooed most black Americans to them, and implementing the program of negrophilia, it created an atmosphere in which blacks' political position is sacrosanct. If one criticizes a black person's political allegiance, they are accused of wishing to see blacks segregated or even enslaved again, since it was the political process that was used to ensure parity, by and by.

In his August 13, 2008, column for the *Wall Street Journal*, Jeffrey Lord enumerated certain points that I and others have been making for years. In the column, Lord addressed the hypocrisy of the Democratic Party's history pertaining to race relations—which is blatant propaganda—as represented on its Web site:

- There is no reference to the number of Democratic Party platforms supporting slavery. There were six from 1840 through 1860.
- There is no reference to the number of Democratic presidents who owned slaves. There were seven from 1800 through 1861.
- There is no reference to the number of Democratic Party platforms that either supported segregation outright or were silent on the subject. There were 20, from 1868 through 1948.
- There is no reference to "Jim Crow" as in "Jim Crow laws," nor is there reference to the role Democrats played in creating them. These were the post-Civil War laws passed enthusiastically by Democrats in that pesky 52-year part of the DNC's missing years. These laws segregated public schools, public transportation, restaurants, rest rooms and public places in general (everything from water coolers to beaches). The reason Rosa Parks became famous is that she sat in the "whites only" front section of a bus, the "whites only" designation the direct result of Democrats.
- There is no reference to the formation of the Ku Klux Klan, which, according to Columbia University historian Eric Foner, became "a military force serving the interests of the Democratic Party." Nor is there reference to University of North

Carolina historian Allen Trelease's description of the Klan as the "terrorist arm of the Democratic Party."

- There is no reference to the fact Democrats opposed the 13th, 14th and 15th amendments to the Constitution. The 13th banned slavery. The 14th effectively overturned the infamous 1857 Dred Scott decision (made by Democratic pro-slavery Supreme Court justices) by guaranteeing due process and equal protection to former slaves. The 15th gave black Americans the right to vote.

- There is no reference to the fact that Democrats opposed the Civil Rights Act of 1866. It was passed by the Republican Congress over the veto of President Andrew Johnson, who had been a Democrat before joining Lincoln's ticket in 1864. The law was designed to provide blacks with the right to own private property, sign contracts, sue and serve as witnesses in a legal proceeding.

- There is no reference to the Democrats' opposition to the Civil Rights Act of 1875. It was passed by a Republican Congress and signed into law by President Ulysses Grant. The law prohibited racial discrimination in public places and public accommodations.

- There is no reference to the Democrats' 1904 platform, which devotes a section to "Sectional and Racial Agitation," claiming the GOP's protests against segregation and the denial of voting rights to blacks sought to "revive the dead and hateful race and sectional animosities in any part of our common country," which in turn "means confusion, distraction of business, and the reopening of wounds now happily healed."

- There is no reference to four Democratic platforms, 1908-20, that are silent on blacks, segregation, lynching and voting rights as racial problems in the country mount. By contrast the GOP platforms of those years specifically address "Rights of the Negro" (1908), oppose lynching (in 1912, 1920, 1924, 1928) and, as the New Deal kicks in, speak out about the dangers of making blacks "wards of the state."

- There is no reference to the Democratic Convention of 1924, known to history as the "Klanbake." The 103-ballot convention was held in Madison Square Garden. Hundreds of delegates were members of the Ku Klux Klan; the Klan so powerful that a plank condemning Klan violence was defeated outright. To celebrate, the Klan staged a rally with 10,000 hooded Klansmen in a field in New Jersey directly across the Hudson from the site of the convention. Attended by hundreds of cheering convention delegates, the rally featured burning crosses and calls for violence against African-Americans and Catholics.

- There is no reference to the fact that it was Democrats who segregated the federal government, at the direction of President Woodrow Wilson upon taking office in 1913. There is a reference to the fact that President Harry Truman integrated the military after World War II.

- There is reference to the fact that Democrats created the Federal Reserve Board, passed labor and child welfare laws, and created Social Security with Wilson's New Freedom and FDR's New Deal. There is no mention that these programs were created as the result of an agreement to ignore segregation and the lynching of blacks. Neither is there a reference to the thousands of local officials, state legislators, state governors, U.S. congressmen and U.S. senators who were elected as supporters of slavery and then segregation between 1800 and 1965. Nor is there reference to the deal with the devil that left segregation and lynching as a way of life in return for election support for three post–Civil War Democratic presidents, Grover Cleveland, Woodrow Wilson and Franklin Roosevelt.

- There is no reference that three-fourths of the opposition to the 1964 Civil Rights Bill in the U.S. House came from Democrats, or that 80% of the "nay" vote in the Senate came from Democrats. Certainly there is no reference to the fact that the opposition included future Democratic Senate leader Robert Byrd of West Virginia (a former Klan member) and Tennessee Senator Albert Gore Sr., father of Vice President Al Gore.

Last but certainly not least, there is no reference to the fact that Birmingham, Ala., Public Safety Commissioner Bull Connor, who infamously unleashed dogs and fire hoses on civil rights protestors, was in fact—yes indeed—a member of both the Democratic National Committee and the Ku Klux Klan.

Here's this line from the DNC: "With the election of Harry Truman, Democrats began the fight to bring down the final barriers of race . . ." Truman, of course, was elected in 1948, and to his great credit he did in fact, along with then-Minneapolis Mayor Hubert Humphrey, begin to push the Democrats towards a pro-civil-rights stance. This culminated in the passage of the 1960s civil rights laws—legislation that redid what had been done by Republicans a hundred years earlier but undone by the Democrats' support for segregation. But the notion that "Democrats began to bring down the final barriers of race" raises the obvious questions. What were these barriers doing there in the first place? And who exactly was responsible for creating them?

As if to confirm the "Who, me?" racial psychology behind the DNC Web site, Nancy Pelosi's Democrats passed a House resolution on July 29 sponsored by Tennessee Democrat Steve Cohen. The resolution, passed by voice vote, concludes this way:

Resolved, That the House of Representatives

(1) acknowledges that slavery is incompatible with the basic founding principles recognized in the Declaration of Independence that all men are created equal;

(2) acknowledges the fundamental injustice, cruelty, brutality, and inhumanity of slavery and Jim Crow;

(3) apologizes to African Americans on behalf of the people of the United States, for the wrongs committed against them and their ancestors who suffered under slavery and Jim Crow; and

(4) expresses its commitment to rectify the lingering consequences of the misdeeds committed against African Americans under slavery and Jim Crow and to stop the occurrence of human rights violations in the future.

What word is missing here?
You got it. The word "Democrat."[3]

So why belabor the point? Certainly, whichever party was unlucky enough to have that track record would be ashamed at this juncture in our history. Why does it matter?

It matters because:

1. They're *not* ashamed,
2. The machinations by which the Dixiecrats (and later the far left) within the party conspired to subjugate the black community and the black vote are among the greatest evils perpetrated upon a people since slavery and Jim Crow, and which, by the way, *are still being perpetrated*, and
3. *They* helped to construct the apparatus of negrophilia.

By the middle of the Civil Rights Movement, many Americans, black and otherwise, believed that the nation owed some form of restitution in the area of assistance, a "counteractive" to the decades of segregation, Jim Crow, and general inequity. In theory, this was an appropriate posture. Unfortunately, this translated into guilt and power-driven social programs being implemented. These helped to change the face of black families, demographics, and the educational, industrial, and corporate worlds—often, not for the better.

In the interest of political power, particularly left-leaning, Northern state legislatures facilitated liberal (no pun intended) distribution of social welfare resources. From approximately 1910 until the Great Depression, blacks had begun moving into Northern urban areas due to the generally better treatment, voting rights, and job opportunities. During and after Franklin Delano Roosevelt's administrations, union concerns in the North—particularly in cities such as Chicago, Detroit, and New York—began to pressure Democrats with their concerns for blacks (who were relocating into these Northern cities) taking jobs from whites.

The solution killed two birds with one stone. Increased entitlements and broader qualification criteria brought more blacks onto welfare rolls; this not only assuaged the unions' perception of being threatened, but served to acclimatize urban blacks into the culture of dependency that is a pillar of Democratic power to this day.

This practice resulted in an even greater flood of blacks into urban areas from the South. When I was a young child, for a time I wondered why my mother didn't have a Southern accent, because the majority of black people I knew (who at that time were schoolmates) had Southern accents. Everyone I knew, it seemed—who wasn't Italian, Irish, or Jewish—spoke fondly of "back home," which was invariably somewhere in the South.

Here I believe it is essential to include some more of my personal observations and experience, not simply to validate my position, but to provide insight as to some of the factors that allowed negrophilia to insinuate itself into American culture.

The subversion of the black family unit (which is discussed in more detail in the following chapter) facilitated development of the urban black subculture that exists today. The requisites for many forms of public assistance included an absent head of household (usually, the father of children). While black families in urban areas previously reflected the norm for the economically disadvantaged (i.e., a father, mother, and children), men were either encouraged to absent themselves or to remain in the South when mother and children moved to Northern cities. Many of these men came to feel (or believe) they were obsolete, and began to absent themselves completely. Between the perversion of practical aspects of family living and family members often being significant distances apart geographically, relationships suffered. Blacks began to drift in and out of relationships. Women began to have children from multiple partners; this was encouraged by the state, which rewarded them economically.

⁂

Don't you remember I told ya,
I'm a soldier in the war on poverty . . .
—BILLY PRESTON, "Nothing from Nothing," 1974

Despite there now being financial assistance to "compensate" for the evils of segregation and Jim Crow, there was plenty of resentment to go around. Public assistance as primary income provided just enough for subsistence. The federal Aid to Families with Dependent Children (AFDC) program, implemented in 1935, ballooned in its scope and coverage of families headed by single mothers in the 1960s; the majority of these were black women in inner cities. From the late 1960s to 1980, the numbers receiving benefits increased nearly twofold.

Black single-mother families were crowded into tenements or housing projects. Tangential to this, the identical protocol was implemented vis-à-vis former residents of the island of Puerto Rico, a commonwealth of the United States; public assistance was easier to obtain and more plentiful in major American cities than it was on the island. Crime began to flourish, with impoverished blacks preying upon their neighbors. Organized crime was all too willing to ameliorate blacks' discontent with diversions such as gambling, prostitution, and narcotics. Poor but enterprising black men—who became more and more convinced that their lot in life with "whitey" calling the shots was more or less predetermined—became involved in the rackets at the street level. Some became fairly wealthy, if they weren't incarcerated or killed.

Local politicians and activists served to fan the fire of this resentment; what was being provided clearly wasn't enough. Being poor in the South or the North was still being poor, so the trade-offs were dubious. The educational models in these areas were of legendary deficiency (as they remain today); between this factor, children coming from dysfunctional, unstable families, and living in squalid and often dangerous situations, the performance of black students plummeted. There were more opportunities, to be sure, but fewer black students were motivated enough to take advantage of them.

Guilty-feeling whites, whether politicians or the man in the street, yielded time and again to liberal arguments that "the poor" needed more. In major urban areas, the electorate tended to agree. Yet it was never enough and resentment continued to mount.

From 1959 to 2000, levels of black poverty fell 32.6 percent, while the white poverty level fell only 8.6 percent during the same period. The overall poverty level from 1959 to 2000 fell 11.1 percent (U.S. Census Bureau, Historical Poverty Tables). Yet, if you consult the establishment press—or worse, the black press—the United States is still a racially divided, institutionally racist nation. Toward advancing this argument, these media entities commonly turn to the claim that nearly half of our prison inmates are black. They contend that this is a statistical reality, ergo "racist nation."

The leading cause of poverty among blacks (75 percent) and non-blacks (65 percent) is drug abuse (according to a recent NPR/Kaiser/Kennedy School study). Eighty-five percent of black children living in poverty reside in a female-headed household (U.S. Census Bureau Population Survey). There are opportunities for blacks who come from reasonably stable environments, and thus are inclined to take advantage of them, but poor blacks who are locked in the pattern of propaganda, poor education, and the cult of victimization remain a subculture in decline. The reason it isn't improving (and in my opinion, will not) is the necessity for keeping them there. Though there were great social inequities in 1959, there was not a subculture of single black females heading households. This demographic was cultivated by political progressives and career civil-rights activists.

The bottom line: A lot of black Americans remain poor and ignorant because that's the way many politicians and activists want them to remain. They were targeted, above other groups, in part to keep them "in their place," and in part to bolster the numbers of the dependent underclass that would continually vote for those who maintain that underclass materially. When other politicians make overtures toward ameliorating this, they are accused of being racists and seeking to deprive "oppressed" blacks of their due. And so it goes.

In the end, black people did not heroically wrest equality from an unwilling white majority. Many blacks (and others) were indeed heroic, but such sweeping social changes do not happen without superior technology and force of arms (as in whites becoming a preeminent minority in South Africa), or a majority that is already disposed to that change. In America, the latter was the case. It was time, and the white majority, as well as blacks, was aware of this. Factions within government and the activist community, however, sabotaged the agenda.

While whites were being persuaded to yield, blacks were being told that whites were not, and would not, so they were encouraged to keep pushing.

∽

Black influence on the arts in America infused our culture with some badly needed "new blood." Nearly all Americans enjoy and have benefitted from the influence of art that originally emanated from within the black community. Jazz, rock 'n' roll, gospel music, and many forms of dance developed there, and were assimilated (if indirectly at times) by mainstream America. My mother was a dance teacher; she founded an African dance troupe in New York in 1968 that consisted mainly of high school kids from the area in which we lived. African and Afro-Cuban dance and music were an integral part of my artistic and cultural development.

One must, however, make a distinction between this influx of creativity and the faction within the black artistic community that, starting during the same period of time, began to use music, poetry, and literature to promote the Marxist agenda. By the time I took my first literature course in college, the primary text of the course included Amiri Baraka (formerly Leroi Jones, born 1934), the foul-mouthed Marxist pseudo-poet who later became a college professor and poet laureate of the State of New Jersey. This is incidental, of course, inasmuch as every opportunity was invariably exploited and validated the revolutionary aspects of Marxism and intellectually ingratiate Marxists to blacks. This was also ancillary to the far left's infiltration of black churches, which will be covered presently.

While this was taking place, the entertainment industry was going overboard as well. Corporate entertainment (which had indeed merited scrutiny during Senator Joe McCarthy's anti-communist investigations of the 1950s) had been leaning farther to the left with each passing year. It began to create a representation of blacks that would serve the purposes of progressives in propagandizing whites while politicians, activists, and the establishment press manipulated blacks for some of the same ends.

Certainly entertainment—which results in revenue—was a factor. Films and television increasingly began to portray blacks as possessing nothing but positive qualities. In productions in which blacks and whites interacted, whites were often portrayed as possessing an overabundance of negative qualities. This phenomenon became so widespread that comedians began to craft jokes and comedy routines around it.

Heaven help the individual who suggests that a white person might be better at a given activity, whether mentally or physically focused, than a black one. Since blacks began to be accepted in the arena of professional sports, they have excelled, often to the extent of coming to dominate certain sports. It is commonly accepted by many Americans that they are inherently "better" than whites in these areas. *White Men Can't Jump*. It's a given.

What gives truth to this truism is something that progressives would balk at applying to whites, if the shoe were on the other foot.

It's pretty much common knowledge at this point among physiologists, kinesiologists, and bodybuilders that blacks tend to have less intramuscular fat than whites. Why? Because Northern Europeans needed more insulation (to avoid turning into "The Iceman") against the colder climates than did Africans. So blacks tend to have denser, leaner muscle tissue. Bodybuilders have known for decades that white competitors have to get down to a lower percentage of body fat than black competitors in order to get that characteristic (and coveted) chiseled or "cut" look. It is also a likely reason why black athletes dominate sports that require more endurance (long-distance running and basketball) than they do at sports that require short bursts of strength (football, hockey).

So there's a genetic cause for blacks excelling at certain sports; unfortunately, given sensitivities (born of propaganda), one can't make these observations without someone else trotting out accusations of Nazism. Compliment a black athlete and you're either condescending, or you're subtly accusing him/her of being unintelligent, and don't *dare* suggest that whites have any inherent genetic advantages in *any* area.

It is a common contention of some—usually progressives—that blacks and other minorities *cannot actually be racists* because they are not in a position to implement their racism. This convoluted, disingenuous logic is an argument so propagandistic and devoid of common sense that I am strongly inclined, as someone who has experienced bigotry from both whites and blacks, to resolve that such people ought to be summarily stripped of their right to vote, regardless of race.

✐

An interesting phenomenon that I've encountered during the course of writing this book is the lovely object lessons that have presented themselves. If I didn't know better, I'd almost say that they were occurring for my convenience. What's more likely, of course, is that negrophilia is so common and so ingrained in our worldview at this point that the sorts of things one would point to in arguing for its existence just happen so damned frequently that it isn't very difficult to identify them—particularly if one is looking.

On July 16 of 2009, during a congressional Environment and Public Works Committee hearing, Harry C. Alford, the president and CEO of the National Black Chamber of Commerce, accused Senator Barbara Boxer of being racially condescending to him. Alford had opposed a climate-change bill that passed in the House of Representatives, contending that the bill would have deleterious effects on small and minority-owned businesses.

Senator Boxer, chair of the committee, retorted with a quote from an NAACP resolution that approved the bill. When Alford accused the senator of being condescending, Boxer—a committed leftist—suggested she might quote yet another black organization that had approved the measure.

While Alford's initial concern regarding the bill was indeed about how it would affect minority-owned businesses, he was ruffled at

Boxer's inference that since other black organizations had approved of the bill, he ought to as well. He then became irate, claiming that she was making race the issue. Indirectly, that was true; actually, she was making race *conformity* the issue. The minority organizations that approved the bill were in lockstep with congressional leftists; this conformity is the stock-in-trade between minorities and progressive power players. If minority-owned businesses were going to be adversely affected by the bill in question, it was a sacrifice that ought to be made for the benefit of far-left objectives. As benefactors of their largesse, minorities are expected to conform without protestation to whatever the aforementioned power players dictate.

The exchange between Alford and Boxer was a perfect example of racism on the part of progressives—which, as may surprise some, *is actually an aspect of negrophilia.*

I shall explain: In my experience, among politically active people, I have always seen more evidence of racism among those on the left. In the shallow, superficial view of progressives, they feel (rather than *think*) that the outward show of a sense of justice as regards race issues is somehow important. Consequently, they have contrived all sorts of devices—negrophilia among them—in order to maintain this façade. Among the power players, there is always more in it for them; rank-and-file progressives just get to feel really good about the perceived value of what they are supporting.

Reciprocity is always expected. Among many progressives, it may not even be a conscious thing. When it comes down to contentious issues, however, whether it be between a customer and a store clerk, a supervisor and an employee, or the member of a business interest and a U.S. senator, the unspoken quid pro quo is always present: *After all we've done for you, you'd damn well better just shut up and keep your place.*

FIVE

religion

*I have said my master found religious sanction for his cruelty.
As an example, I will state one of many facts going to prove the
charge. I have seen him tie up a lame young woman, and whip her
with a heavy cowskin upon her naked shoulders, causing the warm
red blood to drip; and, in justification of the bloody deed, he would
quote this passage of Scripture—"He that knoweth his master's will,
and doeth it not, shall be beaten with many stripes." Master would
keep this lacerated young woman tied up in this horrid situation
four or five hours at a time. I have known him to tie her up early in
the morning, and whip her before breakfast; leave her, go to his store,
return at dinner, and whip her again, cutting her in the
places already made raw with his cruel lash.*
—From *Narrative of the Life of Frederick Douglass, an American Slave*

THAT WHICH POSSESSED African slaves to adopt "the religion of
their masters" is barely fathomable to the twenty-first century
American who has lived a life of freedom and comfort. One might
presume that they would want nothing whatsoever to do with the so-
called faith that allowed for cruel psychopaths among the religious
men who had enslaved them. But accept Christianity they did, and
almost universally.

The religious practices Africans brought to North America varied,
owing to the diverse backgrounds of the people concerned. The religions of West Africa (from whence most of these Africans came) primarily included dozens of forms of animism, spiritism, and syncretistic
faiths. These are commonly referred to as "indigenous" religions.

Many of these religions, such as the Akan (a major religion in Ghana, Benin, the Ivory Coast, Togo, and the Congo), are syncretistic, including countless deities, animal sacrifice, and spirit possession. Vodun, a religion that is still practiced by many millions of people in West African nations, is the religion from which Voodoo takes its name.

In certain areas, key aspects of these religions were carried over into slaves' Christian practices, giving rise to such faiths as Santeria and Voodoo; in other instances, slaves more or less made a straight trade, as it were, for Christianity. As time went on, unless there happened to be groups of slaves in significant numbers from the same immediate region, native religions were lost through attrition; if there was no one to keep the faith alive, it fell by the wayside.

The motives for slave owners toward desiring their slaves to be Christians varied. It is likely that many believed that the more black slaves conformed to the "norm," the more harmoniously they would function within the culture. "Keeping them in line" might be a more accurate idiom for this practice. It is possible that this was simply a perfunctory effort toward "civilizing" their slaves, and the long-term ramifications were not considered.

Perhaps some slave owners reasoned that faith in Christ might make the lot of their charges somewhat more bearable. How these slave owners were able to reconcile the hypocrisy of owning slaves in the first place is irrelevant; the fact is that many did, and it did not necessarily make them monsters. As recorded in the Gospels, certain members of the early church were themselves slaves, and the New Testament contains references to how such persons might live obediently but with dignity, and without despairing their lives away.

Then there were those who did not wish their slaves to be Christians—and particularly to study the Gospels. Many slave owners believed that blacks were simply not intelligent enough to grasp the contents thereof and the concepts of Christian faith, and that attempting to instruct them in it would be a waste of time better spent working.

Then there was the fear factor. Slave owners who did not wish their slaves to adopt Christianity presumed that any knowledge beyond what would make slaves useful was potentially dangerous. Among other things, studying the Gospels presented the danger that some slaves might learn how to read and put themselves more on a par with whites. There are many writings that have survived from the era of slavery that depict slaves going to great lengths, and at the risk of severe punishment, to study the Gospels. Frederick Douglass's writings are among those that include such subject matter. In retrospect, he was probably a prime example of what blacks might do were they to become lettered people. Not only were such blacks able to reason their way around whites, but they were able to hold their Christian masters' hypocrisy up before them. Much of this was occurring during a time in which the American colonies were themselves developing; between taming a frontier, conflicts with natives (Native Americans), exploitation by the British Crown, and day-to-day concerns, Christianizing their slaves was probably not foremost on their minds. "But clergy were in short supply even for whites in the eighteenth-century South. In 1701 Virginia, for example, only half of the forty-some parishes containing 40,000 people were supplied with clergy. And regarding white settlers in Georgia, one missionary said, 'They seem in general to have but very little more knowledge of a Savior than the aboriginal natives.'"[4]

The reason or reasons as to how or why black slaves embraced Christianity would likely give rise to lengthy discussion. As a Christian, I am biased, and tend to lean toward spiritually based reasons, along with the quality of Christ's message. Whatever the case, black slaves did embrace Christianity, and with a fervor. Many became deeply religious; when not otherwise occupied, they could be seen in prayer or reading the Bible. Some practiced fasting and, despite the admonitions of those slave owners who eschewed Christianizing their slaves, held secret Bible studies and services away from prying eyes.

In 1831, a Virginia slave named Nat Turner came to the conclusion that God wished him to deliver blacks in the United States from slavery via armed rebellion. He led an uprising that resulted in fifty-five deaths. Given the religious overtones of the rebellion, laws were passed making it illegal for blacks to preach or engage in autonomous assembly.

Here, I find it necessary to admonish modern American Christians. Apart from having gravitated away from sincere faith, whether by choice or the prevailing zeitgeist, I perceive that there are altogether too many Americans who call themselves "Christian" with whom Frederick Douglass would have a field day. Indeed, one of the chief arguments put forward by the evangelical community today is that many Christians—perhaps the majority in the United States—are people for whom Christianity is a quaint convention and a form of social intercourse. There are very few precepts of the faith to which these people adhere; to them, the concept of a resurrected Christ is as alien as it is to most agnostics. The adage "the problem with Christianity is Christians" is a sad testimony to this fact. Granted that this is an ancillary issue to which many volumes could be devoted; suffice it to say that the deficiencies of American Christians—often stemming from arrogance—bear much of the blame for blacks' struggles in America, from the antebellum South to this day.

∽

The white God is an idol, created by the racist bastards,
and we black people must perform the iconoclastic task of
smashing their false images.
—JAMES CONE, *A Black Theology of Liberation*

Black Liberation Theology (BLT) was concocted by Dr. James H. Cone, who was born and raised in Arkansas. He received a BA degree from Philander Smith College and his PhD degree from Northwestern University in 1965. Like many people at that juncture in our history, he was concerned with contemporary issues as well as the lot of blacks in America. At some point, the issues at hand—women's issues, racism, and so forth—began to affect his theology, rather than the reverse. While another might have sought to superimpose the Christian ethic upon an unjust society (as did Dr. King), he sought to change the church. His adoption of Marxism and utilizing it to woo black Christians was likely born of frustration; his faith was probably further subverted in the various universities he attended and in which he taught. This was the fate of quite a few black professors and, of course, hundreds of thousands of black students of the Civil Rights Era. The anomalous aspect here is that most who went this way leaned more toward the secular or were Christians who abandoned the church altogether.

Cone's 1969 book, *Black Theology and Black Power*, presented a perverted and wholly un-Christian view of the black church. His exegesis and subsequent hermeneutics in the formulation of BLT might as well have been done on LSD. In the practical sense, Black Liberation Theology is but one of many devices adopted by the far left in order to divert black Americans from their faith and from allegiance to their country and its founding precepts.

As far as all conventionally accepted paradigms of Christianity go, Black Liberation Theology is nothing less than apostasy. BLT perverts the liberation of the individual from sin (egoism) and the world (prioritizing of the non-spiritual) into a militant racist message of liberation from earthly (in this case, white) oppressors, and speaks to an exalting of blacks (although it could just as easily reference any race) above all others. It advocates a spiteful and conceited rejection of a deity that will not subscribe to the believer's notion of what He ought to be doing for them, vis-à-vis unfettering His worshippers. This central message of liberation—which is most assuredly *not* what Christ advocated—is pure Marxism. This ought not be surprising, as it was conceived by a man who had an affinity for Marxism, and was refined by others who were outright Marxists. Ironically, of course—as anyone who has studied Marxism realizes—*the liberation that their adherents look for is nonexistent;* the promise of deliverance is just the carrot Marxist leaders employ to secure power. The stick is later turned upon devotees in order to beat them into total submission.

Sadly, in their quest for a distinctive identity, many black Americans, including quite a few ministers, fell prey to the blasphemous creed of Black Liberation Theology.

> *The fact that I am Black is my ultimate reality . . . it is impossible*
> *for me to surrender this basic reality for a "higher, more universal"*
> *reality. Black theology knows no authority more binding than the*
> *experience of oppression itself.*
> —JAMES CONE, *Black Theology and Black Power*

Since 2007, when I first revealed the association between then-Senator Obama and Black Liberation "theologist" Rev. Jeremiah Wright, and particularly since the airing of Wright's vitriolic sermon excerpts, certain biblical scholars and real theologians have seized upon the opportunity to publicly compare and contrast BLT with mainstream Christianity. As it happens, there was a substantial amount of information available on the subject prior to 2007; now there's little doubt it didn't get nearly the amount of attention it merited.

One essay that has gained exposure over the last couple of years is *The Truth About Black Liberal Theology*, by Dr. Robert A. Morey, founder of the California Biblical University and Seminary in Irvine, California. Morey's study is probably the most direct and succinct primer on the subject.

> *The fundamental ideas of BT did not come from black thinkers but from such white European thinkers as Hegel, Darwin, Marx, etc. It is Euro-centric in its ideology although it is Euro-phobic in its rhetoric. Black liberal theologians are in reality "Uncle Toms" still licking the boots of their white, Marxist masters at such bastions of white liberalism as Princeton, Yale, Harvard, etc.*
> *They are the slaves of Karl Marx.*
> —DR. ROBERT A. MOREY, *The Truth About Black Liberal Theology*

The commentary above supports the point I've made many times in response to those who claim that black conservatives are Uncle Toms, race traitors, and things of this nature: Black civil-rights activists (BLT proponents included) have long since been corrupted by the agenda of far-left whites, an agenda that has done infinitely more harm to black Americans than good. The individuals who engage in BLT's racist invective seldom have a solid working knowledge of the history of the United States, but with BLT, pundits and pastors are validated with an almost unlimited supply of credentials toward promoting this insidious movement.

More damaging, black pastors, in and out of BLT churches, have allowed the secular agenda of the left to thoroughly permeate their churches, and consequently, black culture. Think about that the next time you see a poor, unwed, pregnant teenage black girl.

The goals of BT are to turn religion into sociology,
Christianity into a political agenda, Jesus into a black Marxist rebel,
and the gospel into violent revolution. They are more interested in
politics than preaching the gospel.
—Dr. Robert A. Morey, *The Truth About Black Liberal Theology*

This is evidenced in just about all of the video excerpts of Rev. Wright that were broadcast; Wright, Rev. James Meeks (another Obama BLT associate), and Rev. Otis Moss (Wright's successor) seem wholly invested in accentuating the negative in every meaningful area of blacks' lives, from their self-perception, to their worldview, to the evil of their "oppressors."

A brilliant study of BLT was done in several essays and a dissertation by Anthony B. Bradley, an assistant professor of theology at Covenant Theological Seminary in St. Louis, Missouri. Excavating the roots of BLT, from Jeremiah Wright's beloved James Cone, the chief architect of Black Liberation Theology, to the contextual present, Bradley explains how BLT is about as far from New Testament Christianity as it could be.

Pastors such as Wright speak of "the black Church," but there is no black Church, or white Church, or any-other-ethnicity Church if the discussion remains confined to Bible-based Christianity. The salvation of Christ transcends ethnicity, period. Those who embrace hatred, racism, judgment, etc., shrouded by Christian trappings are either spiritually immature or have a disingenuous and malignant agenda.

The "black religious tradition" referenced by Wright and other BLT proponents is not traditional, unless one counts the Marxist-infused "tradition" established in the sixties. Certainly, black Christian Americans' experiences have been socially and spiritually unique unto them. BLT's "black church" as a cultural phenomenon, however, is not the church that maintained blacks through the ignominy of slavery and segregation, bringing them through these not only with a sense of dignity, industry, and self-worth, but grasping the Gospel with far more dedication and understanding than many whites.

Like many black Americans, I never heard the kind of swill proffered by Rev. Wright in a black church, and so did not identify BLT with churches in which the congregants were predominantly black. One might wonder why black pastors themselves do not speak out against BLT.

The fact is that, occasionally, they do. Take the story of Rev. Lainie Dowell, a Five-Fold minister from Columbia, Maryland, with a long history in the church and very impressive credentials in her own right.

When it was not popular to do so, twenty years ago, I spoke out against the same kinds of rantings about white people preached by my black pastor and other black colleagues. In an attempt to intimidate me and shut me up, he conspired with cohorts and filed false police reports and court documents to have me arrested inside the church.
—REV. LAINIE DOWELL, April 17, 2008

So much for the question of why black pastors might not challenge BLT; gangsterism and conspiracies to discredit enemies using the law and the press are right out of the Marxist playbook. Being arrested inside one's own church would likely stand as a pretty dissuasive example for a dissatisfied member of the clergy. For the record, Rev. Dowell's pastor (also named Wright, but no relation to Jeremiah) not only preached Black Liberation Theology, but had a strikingly similar religious background to Trinity United's Rev. Jeremiah Wright.

When challenged by laypeople, these pastors become belligerent and switch to "Pharisee mode"—pointing to their credentials, their degrees, the contention that no one but they can understand black religious and social history in America and relate it to a black congregation. We already have an example of their modus operandi when challenged by colleagues, and I certainly have experienced the fruits of my own challenges. For months after I exposed the Obama/Wright connection on Fox News, Wright dedicated an entire page on Trinity United Church's Web site to discrediting me by name.

Finally: The incongruence with mainstream Christianity aside, Black Liberation Theology doesn't even make sense. Churches and pastors that espouse BLT could not exist without one essential element: a white oppressor. The more one studies this heresy, the clearer it becomes that this element is even more important than Christ Himself.

Where then, one may ask, is the salvation of Christ in this theology? Theoretically, let us suppose that we awake one morning to find that everyone is black. Who is the oppressor then? Where is BLT's credibility? They seem to know who their enemy is *now*; however, it isn't the same one that Christians at large acknowledge.

Dr. Morey maintains that BLT is of that enemy, the Devil. Many Christians agree. Non-Christians may view it as general corruption of the church as an institution of cultural stability. For practical purposes, the calculated outcome is the same.

In parts of America, there are enclaves of white supremacists who embrace forms of "Christianity" that foster perverted, quasi– Old Testament views of black Americans as latter-day Canaanites or the cursed descendants of one of Noah's errant sons. Some other doctrines are even more bizarre. I would wager that 99 percent of whites in America find this as disgusting as I do. I submit that Black Liberation "theologians" ought to be viewed in precisely the same light, as both extremes are undeniably racist and can have nothing but deleterious effects on the harmonious progression of American society.

Perhaps, as some assert, clerics among black activists are to be condemned to a greater degree than secular activists for prostituting faith, but the motivation and the result remains the same in nearly all instances. Whether Jeremiah Wright or Jesse Jackson, these are examples of the exploitation of people for personal gain; in this case, the people happen to be black. There is a great deal of sensitivity surrounding the issue of how blacks have been treated in America, but we must remember that a great deal of this sensitivity has been capitalized upon, exacerbated, and protracted by these so-called advocates for blacks. Hence, the term "poverty pimps," as they do nothing but enrich themselves at the cost of those they claim to serve.

And this cost? Look around. The black family a joke, poverty, atrocious rates of school dropouts, incarceration, and unwed mothers, yet everything that perpetuates these—bohemian culture, rap music, promiscuity, victimhood, and defiance—is held as sacrosanct. Can't take those away from blacks, unless one wants to be accused of racism or of being a race traitor.

Such a lovely racket they have . . .

To churches in the 1950s and 1960s, "social justice" (in addition to never being capitalized) meant that those of the Christian faith had the responsibility for implementing the tenets of that faith in the area of promoting equality for blacks. Now, the term means paying homage to the Marxist tenets of liberation theology, and essentially allowing BLT pastors and other leaders of the far left to set the agenda for social issues. These "issues" ostensibly include poverty, incarceration rates, education, and the like, but are truly dedicated to promoting Marxist social order through the current progressive social engineering machine. Elucidation upon these concepts may be gained through the journal *Social Justice*, an overtly Marxist quarterly that was founded in 1974.

Like so many before him, President Barack Obama pays lip service to ameliorating these problems; still he remains intractably on the side of those who have stroked blacks with one hand while repeatedly stabbing them with the other, ever since the Civil Rights Movement began. Given Obama's track record prior to becoming a candidate, there was no reasonable expectation that he would perform any differently if elected president. During the 2008 election campaign, he accused his detractors of trying to scare voters where he was concerned. Though the facts about him ought to have horrified them, they remained oblivious with the press acting as Obama's surrogate.

As scholars and genuine theologians have determined, Black Liberation Theology is but one thing: a perversion of Christianity intended, by design, to woo blacks from faith and toward Marxist thought. "Blackness" is to be worshipped, as is the state—another manufactured intangible—in Marxism. Having established this deification of ethnicity, as far as leftist puppet masters go, the sky's the limit.

Black Liberation Theology would never have evolved, let alone gained a significant foothold within the black religious community, had it not been for negrophilia. Between the First Amendment dictating a "hands-off" policy regarding religious institutions (even if they were radical and cultish), and the emerging inordinate tolerance of all efforts to make restitution to black Americans, BLT was allowed to flourish. Radical Marxist creatures like James Cone were allowed to subvert the black church and ply blacks with their spirit poison. The counterintelligence efforts of the FBI's J. Edgar Hoover, which were applied to black activists pretty much died with him, so tabs the government had been keeping on them expired.

Had the phenomenon of negrophilia been factored out of the equation, BLT would have been viewed by government and society as the dangerous cult that it is. Mainstreaming BLT churches would have been out of the question, and the majority of blacks would view men like Cone and Wright as most whites view Warren Jeffs, the jailed pedophiliac president of the Fundamentalist Church of Jesus Christ of Latter Day Saints.

∽

I suppose I would be considered remiss if I excluded a discussion of the phenomenon of Kwanzaa. I resist doing so, the reasons being that:

1. I cannot include within these pages every inane policy, proposal, and convention that has come down the pike as they relate to black Americans; there are simply too many, and
2. Kwanzaa is such an idiotic and indulgent sham that, in my view, it ought not even be dignified with recognition.

Kwanzaa, is—if the reader has not heard—a holiday celebrated primarily in the United States. It is a celebration of African heritage by black Americans that is observed between December 26 and January 1, and involves the lighting of candles, pouring of libations (beverage offerings to deities), feasting, and the exchange of gifts.

"Kwanzaa" is a Swahili word meaning "matunda ya kwanza," or "first fruits." The choice of Swahili (as covered here, the Africans

brought to the Americas during the slave trade spoke scores of languages), in this case, was completely arbitrary. Kwanzaa claims to promote the *Nguzo Saba* (also Swahili), or "Seven Principles," which are ostensibly calculated to encourage community and family values. In themselves, there is nothing wrong with these values, which include such things as unity, creativity, and faith, to name a few; they are in no way exceptional or superior to Christian values (which most black Americans embraced until white progressives got a hold of them), or those advanced in traditions considered to be uniquely American.

In short, it's a bunch of separatist, Afrocentric crap.

As with most of the indulgent stupidity foisted upon black Americans by progressives both black and otherwise, few people sought to criticize or condemn the advent of Kwanzaa, lest they come under fire themselves.

Here comes the good part: Kwanzaa is not, and never has been, rooted in any particular African religious or spiritual tradition. With the exception of the Seven Principles (which bear a strange resemblance to Trinity United Church's Black Value System), Kwanzaa was the brainchild of one Ron Karenga, who was a 1960s black nationalist and FBI informant. Karenga's leanings were Marxist; his organization, the Organization Us, was a bitter rival of the Black Panthers.

Karenga, who was born Ronald Everett in 1941, now goes by *Dr. Maulana* Karenga (having received his PhD in black nationalist studies in 1976). He once served time in prison for assault and kidnapping—a step down from the original charge (the murder of two Black Panthers).

In 1966, Karenga basically invented Kwanzaa as an alternative holiday celebration for disaffected blacks. In recent years, Karenga has resurrected Organization Us, from which his Kawaida Institute of Pan-African Studies sprang. The "Official Kwanzaa Web Site" (officialkwanzaawebsite.org) explains Kwanzaa, but also smacks of sixties social justice rhetoric, black racism, and Marxism. The Kawaida organization, incidentally, is unapologetically Marxist and racist, according to Karenga's own words. It holds seminars and lectures featuring Karenga and all things Afrocentric. Among some Kwanzaa celebrants,

and hardcore Afrocentrics, this throwback is considered some sort of legendary statesman.

As far as religion goes, while Kwanzaa is not a religious celebration per se; it was obviously calculated to supplant the conventional paradigms to which black Americans were familiar, make black Americans feel more African and less American, as well as, of course, *less Christian*. We can't forget that we're dealing with a Marxist (Karenga) here. It does bear mentioning that there remain millions of Christians in Africa itself, many of whom regard Kwanzaa as ridiculous, as do I.

∽

No discourse on religion as pertains to blacks in America would be complete without addressing the Nation of Islam. This sect was founded in the early 1930s by Wallace Fard (Muhammad). He is held by Nation members as having been something on the order of Jesus Christ—only Muhammad was "the real thing."

Fard was actually born in New Zealand in 1891, and emigrated to the United States in 1913. Within a few years, he had been charged with several crimes, among them Prohibition and narcotics violations. After a stint in San Quentin, he moved to the Midwest and finally wound up in Detroit, where he founded the "Lost-Found Nation of Islam in North America." In 1934, Fard went the way of the itinerant carny barker; he disappeared and was never seen nor heard from again. I shall leave speculation as to his fate up to the reader. He is referred to in Nation of Islam circles as simply "He," "Him," or "The Master."

During his time at the helm of the fledgling Nation of Islam, he encountered a young man from Georgia who had moved to Detroit, Elijah Poole, who became one of Fard's original disciples. Poole subsequently wound up doing nearly all of the real work in building the Nation of Islam, traveling across America and setting up mosques. He is held among Nation of Islam members to be (at least) a prophet on the order of Brigham Young of the Mormon Church.

Militancy has always been one of the Nation of Islam's core beliefs. America was founded as the white man's paradise; blacks were brought here to be their slave race. There is little in the Nation's

canon that does not suggest that all whites are inherently evil, evil in a way that transcends any conditioning, education, or enlightenment. The Nation of Islam declares that the moral and cultural paradigm of Africans is superior to that of Northern Europeans (whites). Like other black sects and secular groups, the Nation maintains that blacks ought to renounce Christianity as an instrument of their white oppressors. It is a true subculture, and it has always sought to be.

The premises of the Nation of Islam are very difficult to swallow to anyone with a modicum of education; ironically, the education of blacks in America has always been one of the chief grievances of the Nation. The Nation of Islam holds that American blacks are members of the Tribe of Shabazz from the Lost Nation of Asia, wherever that is. Their doctrine is some of the most bizarre syncretism (with an Islamic basis) that one is likely to come across—perhaps even laughable.

While most Americans have probably never laid their eyes on a member of the Nation of Islam, many urban dwellers have at least encountered a few. The men are usually very well-dressed and professional-looking (usually suits and often bow ties in emulation of their founder), while the women favor modern traditional Muslim attire. The Nation of Islam stresses education (their variety), industry, and obedience. Western vices are eschewed, which has had the effect of reforming many hardened and self-destructive black Americans. Despite this, some members and breakaway or former members do revert to criminality. An example of this is former member Quanell X, one of the leaders in the New Black Panther Party. Quanell (born Quanell Ralph Evans in 1970) is a truly odious self-seeker who advocates violence against whites, whom he still believes are to blame for all blacks' pain.

A socially conservative group (as are traditional Islamic sects), the position of women in the Nation of Islam is one of subordination to men. As such, the duplicity of a man's license to take liberties with women to whom he is not married is sometimes a problem. It has been widely speculated that this (as well as issues of ideology) was among the impetus for the assassination of Malcolm X, who had discovered that (Elijah) Muhammad had fathered at least ten

children out of wedlock, and was threatening to expose him as a philanderer.

An esoteric but nonetheless important aspect of the Nation of Islam is one that a historian or social anthropologist might find noteworthy, but which twenty-first-century, politically correct Americans would be encouraged to ignore: The key leadership of the Nation of Islam has always been light-skinned blacks.

The reasons for this are debatable. In the American black community, light-skinned individuals are not generally shown any particular deference. Working on a basis of individual predilection, light-skinned blacks in America have always been either counted as "just as black" by other blacks (which, for all practical purposes, they were), favored for their complexions, or denigrated for the evidence of their white blood. In the post–Civil War era, many of the lighter-skinned blacks were propertied descendants of slave owners, but were not afforded much latitude in the segregationist South.

In the third world, however, in societies of blacks that included descendants of mulattoes and light-skinned blacks, very often those of lighter complexions became members of favored castes. This has been true even in areas of the West Indies, such as Haiti; there, the light-skinned descendants of French settlers and African slaves dominate the politics and economy to this day, while the majority dark-skinned population lives in legendary squalor.

It appears that the Nation of Islam, in its desire to return to a more "old world," African sociopolitical model, has adopted this paradigm. Whether this is by design, or a matter that the aforementioned social anthropologist might more effectively explain, remains to be seen.

In any case, the sect enjoyed a considerable upsurge in membership during the Civil Rights Movement era, part of which can be attributed to timing, and part to the mission of Malcolm X.

Today, the Nation of Islam is captained by Louis Farrakhan (born Louis Eugene Walcott, in 1933), a former calypso singer. He remains a staunch critic of the United States as a racist, oppressive nation, and routinely turns heads with inflammatory and occasionally anti-Semitic statements. Contrary to the Nation of Islam's commitment to "wisdom, knowledge, and beauty," from their Web site, their leaders have always advocated separatism, and occasionally violence. Whites are faceless devils.

Arguably, all of the trappings of the Nation of Islam might be taken as a mere vehicle for the aggrandizement of its leadership—initially, Elijah Muhammad, and now, Louis Farrakhan. The dogma of the Nation is probably a lot easier to accept when professing same brings one fame, riches, and praise. While due commendation is noted here as to the Nation's practice of keeping blacks from the path of self-destruction, there is no denying that its leadership has always come from the dregs of the black community; the worship of such men and the cultish control exercised from the top down. Despite differences in theology, the leadership of the Nation of Islam and those of the Black Liberation Theology community are known to congregate. Having anti-Americanism and similar rackets in common likely promotes a feeling of fellowship among these factions.

Culturally, given the current zeitgeist, the Nation of Islam is tolerated far more than it should be. It ought to be relegated to cult status, but, due to negrophilia, it is simply seen as another faith to which its adherents are entitled. Louis Farrakhan was voted "Person of the Year" in a Black Entertainment Television (BET) poll.

Considering that ours is a nation that now allows Islamic extremists who are bent on utterly destroying it to hold conferences and establish educational institutions that instruct in Sharia law, this should be of little surprise.

SIX

racism is good

Perhaps it is an unfortunate byproduct of our being a capitalistic society; once upon a time, Americans were (collectively) more able to temper our capitalistic fervor (or greed, if you must) with a sense of moral obligation.

At some point (in the late sixties to early seventies), people within the civil-rights activism community realized that there were conscientious people and institutions willing to support their efforts; indeed, these people had been doing so since the early days of the NAACP. Certain black activists who had earned a name for themselves found that there were many individuals and corporate interests who recognized that making monetary contributions to causes and organizations that (at least ostensibly) furthered the advancement of blacks was excellent public relations.

The industry of civil-rights activism was born.

Obviously, those who had been involved during the Civil Rights Movement had a leg up, as they were already well-known; there would be, however, plenty of room for newcomers. Some of those who had not gone down the road of blatant militancy and self-destruction possessed a great deal of credibility in the black community, as well as with the American public at large. In the main, the press was obliging in facilitating their image-building.

The "greatest" pioneer of this industry has been Rev. Jesse Jackson. Though he had participated in the Selma-to-Montgomery marches in 1965 and served as national director of the Southern Christian Leadership Conference's Operation Breadbasket in Chicago under Rev. Dr. Martin Luther King Jr., his chief claim to fame was having been in close proximity to King's assassination. *He marched with Martin,* so his place in history was secured. He had more or less instant credibility within the black community, politicians, and the press.

Having attained the political power of a community leader, Jackson immediately set about establishing America's biggest civil-rights cash cows. In 1971 he founded Operation PUSH (People United to Serve Humanity), an organization that ostensibly advocated black self-help. In 1984, Jackson initiated the Rainbow Coalition (which later merged with Operation PUSH). Jackson's modus operandi for PUSH was to get major corporations with large presences in the black community to adopt affirmative action programs, provide minority job concessions, and contribute other forms of support to the black community. In the process, Jackson became a multimillionaire.

Leaving aside the question of the dubiousness of promoting affirmative action, Jackson's altruistic motives have frequently been questioned; quite often, successful corporations with any interest at all in being patronized by blacks have found themselves dancing to Jackson's tune. As a result, he is seen in the national business community as an extortionist who uses his influence to blackmail businesses with accusations of discrimination and threats of boycotts. In 1998, Rainbow/PUSH began to harass mortgage lender Freddie Mac for its lending and employment practices. As a result, Freddie Mac pledged to set aside $1 billion in mortgage loans for minorities, *and to donate more than $1 million directly to Rainbow/PUSH.* As we should all be aware, it was pressure such as this that led to the 2008 mortgage lending implosion and subsequent economic recession.

Indeed, Jackson's penchant for shameless self-promotion has been evident since 1968. He was roundly criticized for his appearance on

NBC's *Today Show* the day after King's assassination, due to the fact that he wore the same blood-stained shirt he had worn the day before. How the blood came to be on it has been a matter of contention among King's associates for decades, given that Jackson was in the motel's parking lot when King was shot. Some who were there have even postulated that Jackson went to the balcony and smeared King's blood on it after the shooting. According to aides of King (who were present when the civil rights leader was shot), Jackson's account of events on the day of the assassination, and his own involvement in the aftermath, leave quite a bit to be desired.

Jackson has always been quick to level accusations of individual and institutional racism, even when the allegations are sufficiently dubious as to make the reverend appear unintelligent. Yet due to blind allegiance among blacks and negrophiliacs, somehow he manages to retain a measure of credibility.

In 2001, it was revealed that Jackson had fathered a child out of wedlock with one of his staffers. Rainbow/PUSH wound up paying the mother $15,000 in moving expenses and $21,000 in payment "for contracting work" under the table, for which Jackson was criticized but never sanctioned.

There are two reasons why Jackson's foibles didn't damage his long-term credibility within his circle of influence: One is that nefarious activities are largely tolerated among far-left operatives, a credential Jackson most assuredly holds. While the right is not exempted from such chicanery, it is simply a fact that those rank-and-file members of the right are far more likely to throw their leaders under the bus when they use their positions for personal aggrandizement than those on the left. Indeed, I've heard many rank-and-file members of the left applaud larcenous doings on the part of their leaders, asserting that they would simply love to have had the same opportunity.

The other reason—has this become tedious yet? *Negrophilia.*

As indicated earlier, by the early 1970s, there was still plenty of room for additional operatives in the activism industry tent. In the late 1980s, urban New Yorkers began to hear about a man who, by 2008, would nearly eclipse Jackson in recognition, if not affluence.

Rev. Al Sharpton substitutes infamy for civil-rights credentials. Urban New Yorkers are well-familiar with the mail-order "Reverend" (his bios claim that he was "ordained" at age ten) who came on the scene in 1987 when a fifteen-year-old black girl named Tawana Brawley who'd gone missing was found days later smeared with dog feces and with racial slurs written on her body. After claiming that a gang of policemen had raped her and left her thus, Sharpton took up her cause in the name of highlighting police brutality against blacks (translation: fomenting race hatred and distrust of the police).

Brawley's claims turned out to be false; she'd cooked up the story to evade the consequences of her own questionable activities, that is, punishment from her parents. More importantly, it was determined Sharpton knew this and concealed the fact in his quest to defame the police; Sharpton was in fact found guilty of defamation in a civil court and ordered to pay damages.

Taking a page from Jesse Jackson's playbook, Sharpton quickly put the episode behind him, subsequently involving himself in every remotely race-related media incident in the Big Apple—always loud and accusatory, if barely articulate. Sharpton was heavily criticized for his involvement in protests that followed the 1989 shooting death of a black youth who was attacked by a white mob, and Sharpton was actually stabbed by a drunk during a protest march in Brooklyn in 1991.

This is not to say that he's been on the wrong side of every issue. He organized protests following the racially motivated 1986 Howard Beach slaying of Michael Griffiths and the torture of Haitian immigrant Abner Louima by police in 1997, incidents that ought to have outraged all New Yorkers.

Fomenting race hatred, however (which Sharpton's tirades and derisive tone invariably do), is an imperative for such self-styled "civil-rights" activists, since the presence of race hatred justifies their existence. If you asked New Yorkers (including many blacks) back in the late eighties, most would have told you they considered Sharpton little more than "a fat nigger with a big mouth."

I'm only repeating what I heard . . .

He's slimmed down, to his credit, but the gutter invective and classless, pimpish countenance are still present; his blacks-as-victims rhetoric is still the worst kind of divisive paranoia, and he is now marginally articulate as opposed to barely so (I imagine anyone can improve with years of practice).

The kicker for me is this: Despite Sharpton's rhetoric—which more than suggests that nearly all whites lie awake at night cooking up new ways to screw blacks—it's not as if he was born into a disadvantaged life. Rather, it was the divorce of his parents in 1964 that took Sharpton from middle-class comfort to welfare and housing projects—something that can and regularly does happen to children of all races.

Although this may be a moot point to some, to be fair, Sharpton is no worse than other loudmouthed minority activists. They crave face time on network television; that's fair, since any salesman needs to get his message out. And the message is that America is a racist nation. Doesn't matter if *it's not*—the truth would derail the money train, and they can't have *that* . . .

As nearly everyone from the ivory towers to the mud huts of our planet is aware, in June of 2009, legendary entertainer Michael Jackson died suddenly in what will probably always remain suspicious circumstances. The discussion over his having been hyped versus deserving the artistic accolades he received during his career, and the hype surrounding his demise notwithstanding, his death was like a sock to America's collective gut. Despite his having been a decidedly bizarre individual, he was loved by millions.

Jackson's death provided yet another stellar object lesson in the impudence of America's poverty pimps, Al Sharpton in particular. The ink on the singer's death certificate was barely dry before Rev. Al bulldozed his way into the fray, vying (along with Rev. Jesse Jackson) for face time at Jackson's very big, very public sendoff. Obviously, such a show would validate Sharpton's status as a big gun in the black community. As I write this, I recall how the good reverend made it a point to skulk next to the late soul artist James Brown's casket at the Apollo Theater, after Brown died in 2006, long enough for every photographer in Manhattan to get a shot.

Was Michael Jackson's popularity and the clamor over his passing a function of negrophilia? Though it may surprise some, I don't really believe so. Although Jackson and his brothers became famous during the Civil Rights Movement, the fact that whites became more comfortable with black artists was not only to be expected, but it was a positive thing. Jackson's appeal crossed color lines, and he was tremendously talented. Was he hyped? Yes, but no more that other icons have been. The viral nature of the news of his death can be put down in part to modern technology, which multiplied the effect. There were too many other factors involved— from Jackson's evident preference for the white aesthetic to his eccentricity and legal problems—to significantly credit negrophilia with his fame. Those white Americans who fell prey to negrophilia were probably predisposed to an affinity for the singer, but then so were millions of others for different reasons.

At any rate, Jackson's memorial service was held on July 7, 2009 at the Staples Center in Los Angeles. The event was broadcast around the globe as it occurred, and was viewed by over thirty-one million people. Rev. Al delivered a tacky, stupid diatribe that was on the level of the mongoloids he used to incite to march in New York City. He made it a point of excoriating those—whites, of course—who had criticized Jackson's behavior. This is what made his speech stupid; one would have to be *truly* dense not to see that public censure of Jackson's bizarre conduct over the years was by no means restricted to whites.

It was a clear and gratuitous example of the race hustler capitalizing on a wholly inappropriate venue to hawk his racist wares. "There wasn't nothin' strange about your daddy," Sharpton bellowed into the microphone, addressing Jackson's (white) children. "It was strange what your daddy had to deal with."

Sharpton was referring to racism, of course. In Sharpton's world, there isn't a black person in the United States who hasn't been hung upside down and beaten until they said their name was "Toby" at some point. There isn't anything a black person can do that merits scrutiny, even if it is repeated accusations of child molestation. But that's negrophilia for you. Sharpton completely ignored the fact that the only reason those many thousands of people were present that day was to honor a black man, one who also happened to be one of the most wealthy, successful, and admired Americans in history, for better or worse.

The Michael Jackson memorial fiasco proves beyond a shadow of a doubt—unless one is truly delusional—that Sharpton and those of his ilk will use any and every opportunity to fuel the fires of racial enmity. The world had been Michael Jackson's oyster from the age of ten; when did he ever experience a meaningful episode of racism?

Al Sharpton represents the most gauche example of this depravity. Rest assured, there are many others who simply present themselves more amiably.

Though I consider myself a dedicated capitalist, I believe that an inordinate value placed on money as an object or idol is immoral. It is unfortunate that an analysis of many of the societal evils we face can usually begin with *following the money*. For many years, I made my living in biomedical research. There is a little-known, shameful secret in the industry to which many therein will admit: There is an enormous amount of waste and dishonesty in biomedical research. Some researchers are very much like the trio in the film *Ghostbusters*; for them, research is a meal ticket. Discernible progress in their field of endeavor is the last thing on their minds. After all, what would life-long cancer researchers do if one of them were to find that "magic bullet" that would cure all cancers?

The day civil-rights activism became a viable money-making venture was a profoundly sad day for America . . .

RACISM IS GOOD—AN OBJECT LESSON

Several years ago, the local newspaper for the city in which I live ran an article referencing a community-wide forum on racial issues that had been held a week or so earlier. This forum was similar to many that have been conducted in cities across America. Sponsored by the city's Human Relations Commission, the event had become a matter of sore contention among many residents due to critical and accusatory language bandied about by certain members of the commission.

I believe it is important for Americans to understand the dynamics of institutional "reverse racism" (if you will) as they play out in areas in which they live. Having studied these machinations for years, being a former member of the aforementioned Human Relations Commission and an escapee from the socialist stronghold of New York City, I believe I am in a position to enlighten Americans in this area.

Pertaining to this local race relations forum: On the heels of the newspaper article, the HRC chairman (a black man) and vice-chair (a Latina) resigned their positions due to their perception of the city council's "insensitivity" to the HRC's recommendations regarding race issues. The straw that broke the camel's back, as it were, was the council's opposition to a proposed "human rights protection" ordinance, which many agreed was little more than an end run around the proposed Clear Law Enforcement for Criminal Alien Removal (CLEAR) Act of 2003, a piece of legislation that addressed homeland security issues.

This was no surprise, as the HRC's involvement in supporting the ordinance was initiated by Fuerza Latina, an immigrants' rights group whose stated concern was the possible profiling and subsequent deportation of undocumented Hispanic workers, but whose close alliance with certain Marxist and Hispanic separatist organizations rendered them suspect and the HRC's involvement with them questionable at best.

In a column I wrote for another local paper, I related that one of my pet peeves is the inordinate concern some have for macrocosm issues while ignoring things closer to home; hence my reason for admonishing Americans to pay attention to said issues. What we were seeing was no less than an overture on the part of nonlocal far-lefters to infiltrate local politics. As usual, progressive elements of the media were helping them do it; nearly all of the local press coverage of this issue presupposed grave deficiencies relative to race relations in that city. This was part of the design of which some of the commission members weren't even aware they were a part. In essence, they were being used as pawns by those who wanted to bring every person of color in the city into the entitlement/no-accountability/cult-of-victimization/there's-a-Klansman-behind-every-bush fold, and create an environment in which nothing could be said to or about people of color without the danger of coming under fire—the goal being to cement the influence of the far left in the community.

In areas where a region or municipality has an emerging minority population, the modus operandi typically is as follows:

Phase One—Create a Perception of Widespread or Institutional Racism

This is usually accomplished by capitalizing on the oversensitivity of propagandized minorities and guilty-feeling whites. If you're looking for widespread or institutional racism, try liberal strongholds where minorities are used in the same manner Lenin used the workers. The accusation as it applied to the city I mentioned—one of about one hundred thousand in the Southwestern United States—was patent rubbish.

Members of minority groups are bombarded with rhetoric by liberal whites and black activists asserting that America is fundamentally racist. They come to believe it, adopt an attitude of hopelessness, and subsequently meet with failure in life. Whites are bombarded with rhetoric by liberal whites and black activists asserting that America is fundamentally racist; they are intimidated into shutting up while multiculturalism is rammed down their throats. Some become believers, some become apathetic, and others become resentful, intolerant, and, finally, bigoted. Of course, the resentment that members of said minority groups hold for the white majority evolves into racism, too.

Yes, racism is a good thing . . . for the political left.

Phase Two—Promote Activism

Civil-rights activism is an industry in America, and quite a few opportunists have made a good living at it. The area of race relations is a crucial inroad to securing political power for the left, because communities at large usually relent when faced with the prospect of being labeled as a pack of racists.

I have lived in and spent significant amounts of time in diverse regions of this country, including metropolitan New York and Los Angeles, the Southwest, and parts of the South. I have experienced the effects of discrimination almost everywhere I've been. However, it is my experience that widespread and institutional racism tends to flourish more readily in places where the political left and multiculturalists drive the race politics agenda.

Take New York City, for example. It has (erroneously) been held up as a beacon of brotherhood and tolerance for more than half a century. Yet, Rev. Al Sharpton was actually able to springboard himself into the national spotlight, a very good living, and a run at the Democratic nomination for president in the 1980s by capitalizing on racial tensions there. If one watching the national network news extrapolated from there, of course one would presume that if things were *that bad* in New York City, then things must be positively ghastly everywhere else.

Well, far-left progressives had been running the race politics agenda—along with everything else—in New York for that half-century, so anyone with a modest accompaniment of gray matter can determine who was responsible for the status quo.

The power of these socialists lies in division. Typically, minorities indoctrinated into the culture of hypersensitivity, class envy, and suspicion are rallied; alarmists—usually fairly belligerent ones—from within the minority community are tapped to make repeated and inflammatory community-wide indictments and demands for deference rather than inclusion—and this is what engenders resentment and ultimately bigotry on the part of otherwise open-minded whites and blacks. A complicit media helps to move things handily along.

Phase Two involves the promotion of activism. In the case of the city covered in the discussion of Phase One, the Human Relations Commission completed a report for submission to the city council called "A Comparative Analysis of City Boards and Commissions Diversity and Demographics." The purpose of this was to determine the composition of the city's boards and commissions with respect to ethnicity. The analysis determined that the composition of the city's boards and commissions reflected its demographic almost exactly. I know this because I drafted the report.

This apparently wasn't good enough because one of the goals of the HRC suddenly became to have the city reevaluate its method for seeking minority applications. The commission suggested a target marketing system that focused on distributing board and commission applications to increase minority applicants.

It's been more than suggested that certain forms of activism supplant the religious requirement for some people. The HRC stepped up its meeting schedule, and its meeting minutes reflected the religious zeal I saw emerging during my time with the HRC. The problem was that it was very hard to see the city in question reflected in these discussions. During my tenure there, I witnessed a spirit of an inordinate need to agitate—although I could never quite figure out the reason for its necessity.

Despite good intentions on the part of many concerned, there were marked misconceptions at work within the HRC, and they were readily exploited by socialists from within and without the city. Played out to the conclusion I had seen in other communities, those claiming to have the solution will ultimately create the racial tension they ostensibly seek to eradicate.

Which is exactly what they want.

Phase Three—Legislation . . . and More Legislation

As a Christian person, I believe that the practice of racism is a grievous sin. I realize that claiming this mantle (that of a Christian) isn't popular these days and carries with it a connotation of hypocrisy and intolerance to some, but those who are sufficiently informed will understand why I believe racism is probably as fundamentally antithetical to Christianity as it gets.

At this juncture, I also believe it is prudent to reiterate that I know racism among whites still exists in areas of our nation. The tactic of fomenting feelings of disaffectedness among minority groups of various persuasions and then ingratiating itself to these groups to coalesce its political power is one that has been practiced by the left for at least four decades now, and it is in fact the *cause* of much racism.

Phase Three: Having intimidated whites into the *Good grief! They're going to call us racists! Anything but that!* mindset, the activists, having gained momentum and confidence, approach equally intimidated local government entities. First, various innocuous-sounding initiatives, programs, and forums to "promote diversity"—whatever that means—are offered. But what they are really after is legislation. Ego and a desire to "really accomplish something" will override the good intentions of those with conscientious, if ill-founded, concerns.

Finally, the activists request—nay, demand—that ordinance after ordinance designed to protect "disenfranchised" minority interests be passed. Rooted in hypersensitivity and the cult of victimization, these initiatives run the gamut from civil-rights to criminal to "sanctuary city" issues. Anyone who objects to the process, or any aspect thereof, is labeled a racist.

Incrementally, everything becomes about race. Any and every perceived transgression appears in local media; the more the better if it makes the national news. Trial lawyers (who vote overwhelmingly with the left) start doing very well. If a store clerk is a jerk to someone of color, it must have been because they are a person of color. If a white person has a heated disagreement with someone of color in a public setting, a civil suit results. A minority doesn't get that job over a white competitor? Civil suit. Police become handcuffed with respect to minority perpetrators, generally giving license to same.

Like the Sex Police, who eradicated even the most innocent risqué workplace references with the threat of sexual harassment suits, and the Child Police, who have all but hamstrung parents with regard to disciplining their children, the Race Police bring race to the forefront of every individual's thoughts when they interact with a person of another race.

Clear-thinking, reasonably color-blind individuals might suggest that this result is diametrically opposed to where race relations ought to be going—and they'd be right.

At some point, a charismatic personality emerges to lead the charge; a slick black preacher, perhaps . . . a man of God with nothing but the community and the welfare of his brothers and sisters at heart—like Al Sharpton!

Organizations that are generally known to be liberal bastions are often notoriously exempt from the effect of these initiatives. Such institutions whose elitist, narcissistic administrators routinely discriminate—like universities—are considered well above suspicion. Individuals and, of course, business interests—the larger the better—are the real targets.

It's thought policing, of course; the premise that racism can somehow be truly eradicated via the actions of any agency is infantile. Barring a quantum spiritual leap on the part of humanity at large, racism will be with us for many years to come. It's the phenomenon of the far left perpetuating—and in many cases, creating—racism that should be noted here.

In the face of the machinations I have described, residents simply become more and more divided and resentful.

Phase Four—Nurture the Racism That Now Actually Exists

At this juncture in our history, local news agencies have developed a practice of taking great pains to omit the ethnicity of alleged criminal perpetrators from their reporting. Recently in the city in which I live, a violent home invasion involving gunplay left one perpetrator at large in the community. In the press, no reference whatsoever was given to help the public identify the individual, as doing so would have betrayed his ethnic background, which for some reason has become unacceptable. The practice of this much color-blindness is, in my estimation, sheer lunacy.

Phase Four is what one might call the result of a self-fulfilling prophecy. The majority population who haven't been guilt-tripped into submission get sick of being under constant suspicion, having their beliefs second-guessed, of being berated, legislated against, and publicly criticized so they become resentful of, and finally develop a distaste for, the minority population. They become de facto racists.

About fifteen years ago, in Boulder, Colorado, I had occasion to speak with a young man who had become involved in a white supremacist group. While his views were evidently objectionable, he had not yet become so rabid as to preclude civil conversation. One of the things I found interesting was that a teenage native of such an affluent community would have been susceptible to the overtures of a hate group in the first place, particularly since there were around three black people living in Boulder at the time (I am exaggerating—I think there were five).

As I became more acquainted with race politics and the machinations of the left, it became apparent that this youth had been exposed to the same white-bashing in the media and political arena that I had witnessed over the years, essentially, for all of his life. The culture of victimization works both ways, of course; it becomes as easy for disaffected whites to blame every societal evil on minorities as it is for minorities to blame whites.

At around the time I escaped from New York where I was raised, Al Sharpton was just beginning to rise in popularity—or infamy, if you prefer. He engaged in such activities as high-profile campaigns against the Italian-American community, including news appearances, speeches, and rallies, and marches through ethnic Italian neighborhoods involving thousands of chanting, angry blacks. It was no mystery to me that the relationship between blacks and ethnic Italians, poisoned by years of New York intellectual class warfare propaganda, grew even worse.

It is through these practices that insecure and at-risk communities are inflamed, and how the culture of communities with emerging minority population are poisoned with racism—not due to the wholesale or institutional racism that is purported by activists to exist.

My parents were an interracial couple; when they married, there were still "Whites Only" and "Colored" signs in use in some parts of America. They raised me to have nothing to do with bigots. If everyone simply ostracized people and institutions that practiced racism, before long it would no longer be profitable—socially or economically.

SEVEN

affirmative action

WHEN AFFIRMATIVE ACTION was in its nascent stage, those who saw it for what it was (which we'll get into presently) and opposed implementation of affirmative action guidelines and policies were branded as racists. This standard operating procedure on the part of progressives (lies, intimidation, and schoolyard invective directed at those who oppose them) is a technique that is still being used effectively today. Affirmative action policies were not widely resisted for this reason, and federal equal opportunity laws were passed that served to reinforce many of these policies.

For the record: Affirmative action is a policy or set of policies in which ethnicity or gender are considered in social and institutional settings in order to advance equal opportunity or increase ethnic diversity. Affirmative action took hold in America beginning in the early 1970s. One might say it was a byproduct of the Civil Rights Movement, but this does not mean that its advent was an inevitability. Generally, affirmative action policies addressed employment, education, public contracting, and entitlement programs.

Affirmative action could be put down to good intentions, but as a bureaucratically birthed remedy, it was bound to create more problems than it solved, which is one reason some opposed it from the start. In impulsively attempting to encourage diversity for diversity's sake across all levels of American society, in a way it was like bussing. In many cases, it placed people in places in which they didn't necessarily want to be, and it engendered resentment on the part of people who were already there, or wished to be.

This was at the stage wherein those on the far left really began to gain ground in institutional settings, and in places other than major cities. By the 1970s, the political left already held the territory of academia and public schools; operating upon and promoting the premise that the majority (whites) would likely resist any attempt to promote diversity in every conceivable setting, and having secured the assent of every white soul in America who did not wish to be accused of racism, far-left factions began to insinuate themselves into positions of influence in business and government. There they ensured that affirmative action policies were implemented and enforced, and they were quite creative in the area of coming up with new ones.

The impetus behind affirmative action was twofold: to provide access to advantageous venues in education and employment to minorities and women, along with the presumed benefits thereof, and to rectify disadvantages due to explicit instances of racism or sexism and institutional discrimination.

Though there are millions who concur that affirmative action was an abortion that undercut qualified individuals (primarily in education and the job market) as well as promoting under-qualified individuals, even today there are stalwart proponents of this paradigm of redress. *Affirmative action was, in fact, all about lowering standards* so that blacks (and to a smaller extent, other minorities and women) could compete. The flawed premise: Blacks didn't need the standards lowered so that they could compete; they needed adequate education and a sense of hope and worth, which was in the process of being stultified by the very structure that advocated affirmative action.

As a consequence, programs were initiated wherein students who had no desire to move on to higher education, who had terrible grades, and who had low motivation were given scholarships to universities.

Once there, they studied classes tailored to their abilities (many of them failed these anyway), as well as Marxist-derived ethnic and social studies. Campus groups comprised of indoctrinated affirmative action students sprang up on college campuses across America; in their meetings, they'd sit around, smoke pot, and talk about how whites were ramming it to the black man.

Obviously, in order to accomplish all this, students who were otherwise qualified to be there had to be displaced.

Marginal graduates of substandard high schools and university programs went into the job market. There were countless instances of qualified applicants (mostly white males, but definitely not restricted to them) being turned down for positions due to policies that were established in corporations, government agencies, and the like, in order to satisfy quotas and people like Jesse Jackson, who were liable to descend upon an employer with a lawsuit or boycott.

It was social engineering at its best—or worst, depending on one's point of view.

At present, whether or not a black or minority individual has directly "benefited" from affirmative action policies, many of their credentials can be considered suspect. The incompetence of some is evident at close scrutiny; even in the case of those who are reasonably competent, it is obvious that their education, background, and often their social philosophy is shot through with the residue of far-left dogma. Quite a few journalists (those in the establishment press being excepted) believe this is why then-candidate Barack Obama had certain college records and other documentation from his past sealed.

Thus, there is no comparison between a Dr. Percy Lavon Julian and a Russell Simmons. The former was a genius, a scientist, and altruistic entrepreneur who, when confronted with bigotry, stood his ground like a man (with shotgun in hand, by the way). The latter is a purveyor of destructive pop culture and far-left dogma, a self-seeker who was plainly so indoctrinated into Afrocentrism that, for him, its grasp is all but inescapable.

So, if not affirmative action, then what? Didn't black Americans deserve a "leg up" after enduring the national disgrace of segregation and the attendant bigotry, poverty, and generations of hopelessness? Damned right they did. However, as is typical of bureaucratic fixes—particularly when the agenda is subverted by those who sought to maintain and prolong blacks' misery, and those whose goal was to infect the republic with Marxist ideology—the solutions were patently addled-brained, imprudent, and almost criminally wasteful.

There were aspects of affirmative action that had the potential to be of value. Those policies that promoted the use of black contractors and businesses certainly were sound economic concepts; many of these were likely to contribute more jobs for blacks and resources into black communities. The flies in the ointment, apropos the philosophical premise of affirmative action, however, were the presumptions of white resistance and black incompetence. Then, there was the corruption factor; as noted earlier, such devices ultimately facilitated the insinuation of black civil-rights activists into the process. Their involvement politicized that process and dictated the course of business participation, rather than allowing the market to determine what the most worthy enterprises were. In short, it became an activist-driven, socialist-determined market, rather than a merit-based one.

For an example of what becomes of real reform efforts: In 1996, President Clinton signed the first earnest reform of America's welfare system into law. Workfare—a restructuring of the entitlement system devised by congressional conservatives, but which was actually conceptualized in the late 1960s—provided training and entry-level employment opportunities to those Americans who received welfare benefits (I use the term "benefits" reluctantly). The idea was that, in addition to providing recompense to their fellow Americans for welfare, the recipients could develop or hone skills that would make them more gainfully employable.

The reaction from many inner-city minority welfare recipients was quite passionate. The opportunity to contribute and constructively manage their time, in addition to seeing light at the end of the economic struggle, lifted many up, as well as the self-esteem that came from paying their own way, as it were. Some may recall the profusion of local media accounts that featured such people lauding the programs that were now being geared to actually enhance their lives, as opposed to relegating them to the hopeless hell of living like a lab rat.

As soon as it was implemented, it seemed, the venture was sabotaged by the Clinton administration itself. This was because a significant number of Clinton's supporters on the left balked at the idea. Prosperity and self-sufficiency among black Americans was not something they desired. Far-left elements began to call workfare "slavery," citing that some of the workfare jobs at certain stages of the process did not actually generate a paycheck. Of course, they also called it racist, inasmuch as many of the inner-city beneficiaries of workfare were black. Their campaign to destroy workfare was disingenuous, if not evil, and invertebrate Republicans mutely witnessed workfare's demise rather than be called racists.

The repercussions of affirmative action plague us to this day. In June of 2009, President Obama nominated federal appeals court judge Sonia Sotomayor to the Supreme Court of the United States. Sotomayor is a Puerto Rican and a self-described "product of affirmative action" who was admitted to two Ivy League schools despite scoring lower on standardized tests than her classmates. Upon being nominated, Sotomayor was criticized not only for racist comments she had made in the past, but for a decision involving Connecticut firefighters that many considered to be racially preferential. Critics offered that someone who made such tainted decisions was simply not fit to sit on the Supreme Court. *While the confirmation process was going on,* Sotomayor's would-be colleagues on the Supreme Court ruled that the white and Hispanic firefighters Sotomayor had ruled against as an appeals court judge had been unfairly denied promotions because of their race.

Would it be reasonable to suspect that a judge who was a beneficiary of affirmative action policies might—just might—make biased decisions on issues of race? Of course it would. Further, would it be reasonable to suspect that a judge who had made decisions considered biased (and thus overturned) by the Supreme Court might make other biased decisions on issues of race? Without a doubt.

Yet, here we are. Common sense and any cogent sense of legal and moral obligation would dictate that such a person ought not be nominated, let alone confirmed. America's collective intellect has been so distorted by perverse concepts of parity—including affirmative action, political correctness, and negrophilia—that we have someone who is likely an affirmative action president nominating a racist, affirmative action judge to the highest court in the land, and all is well with the world.

A legally blind man with palsy simply doesn't rise to the level of quarterback for the National Football League—and one used to be able to say with some confidence that boobs simply do not rise to the level of Supreme Court justices. That is what affirmative action was put in place for: so that millions of boobs *could* rise to the level of Supreme Court justices, and any number of other august positions within our society—and swear fealty to the political left.

As if it wasn't bad enough that boobs frequently *do* rise to high levels in our merit-based system due to politics and nepotism . . .

EIGHT

black racism

*T*HIS IS JUST *sad. Your people are dying all over the world and you just trade us in for class and ass. When I see Black people like you I'm reminded of how powerless we are.*

That White man teaches us how to speak like him, think like him, act like him and support his value system.

Please wake up.

The theme of the preceding salvo is somewhat atypical of the hate mail I receive; it usually contains a great deal of vitriol, invective, and profanity. This one, written by a black woman, is, however, pretty typical of the attitudes of lower-middle-class and poor urban blacks. There are, as we will see, even those who are reasonably well-educated and even affluent who also hold these sentiments.

Your people.

I am quite certain that the individual who wrote the above letter (actually, an e-mail) has no idea that her message was a racist one; according to her, I am remiss in not exalting blacks and/or some elusive "black worldview" above all.

Dying all over the world. Yes, blacks are dying all over the world. Well, mostly in Africa. But it isn't whites who are killing them. No—they are killing each other, the same as in our cities. I imagine that white supremacists get an enormous laugh over that one.

Speak like him, think like him, act like him and support his value system. I wonder what this woman might have black people do, given that they are centuries and thousands of miles removed from Africa, genetically hybridized, modernized, and thoroughly a component of American culture and society. Should they engage in tribal warfare? Enslave neighboring social units? Kill each other with machetes? Is the gang warfare among black youth in South Central Los Angeles more representative of how blacks ought to behave than going to college, securing employment, starting businesses, and engaging in civil service?

This was one of the few negative e-mails to which I responded, and only because it was one of the few that wasn't incredibly vile. I reminded the writer that if she thought things were so untenable here, there were plenty of African nations that would simply adore having her support, either as a missionary, a sex slave, or as lunch.

The salient point of this anecdote is that black Americans no longer have a reason to think that way; it is not only preposterous, but astounding that they do. In fact, they think that way because they are *encouraged* to do so. Moreover, whites are encouraged to believe that blacks *have a right* to do so.

A major tenet of negrophilia is that racism on the part of blacks is acceptable, or even proper. Forty years ago, black Americans made a marked distinction between black people and niggers. The latter were, like their white counterparts, those who embraced ignorance, self-indulgence, irreverence, and xenophobia. Self-respecting blacks would no more associate with them than self-respecting whites would associate with neo-Nazi skinheads today.

The professional activists, the press, and the entertainment industry changed all that. Through wordless decree, they pronounced that *all* of America's so-called "black culture" ought to be mainstreamed, no matter how deleterious its effect on the majority of Americans.

Inasmuch as certain politicians and those who counted on black dependency sought to undermine black social institutions, "ghetto" culture was advanced within the black community, particularly among youth. As we have seen, any effort to criticize or curtail this is met with accusations of racism. A prime exemplar is the advent of gangsta rap culture. It is analogous to white honor students and professionals being forced to accept the aforementioned skinheads and illiterate ex-convicts from the Aryan power movement into mainstream society for the sake of ethnic solidarity. The only likely result would be a debasement of the median.

∽

I give interracial couples a look. Daggers. They get uncomfortable when they see me on the street.
—Director Spike Lee

Mr. Lee wouldn't see *me* on the street with my wife for very long after that, as this would require that he be in a conscious state. This man is a perfect example of how black racism is tolerated in America. Every few years, Lee makes a rude, shallow, racist remark in public, yet no one calls him on it because he's black. In an America that had not been programmed with negrophiliac sensibilities, he would lose as much respect (and fans) as Woody Allen did when he first seduced and then married his stepdaughter.

I recall an incident my (white) father used to relate about being in a store with me as a small child and receiving a look of disgust from one middle-aged, middle-class white woman that made him want to disembowel her on the spot. Lee wore an Obama T-shirt during the 2008 campaign, yet obviously holds the same scorn for interracial unions—such as the type that produced me and his candidate of choice. So he's a hypocrite as well.

Spike Lee has done well in life, but he comes from parents who did well too. Ask ten regular filmgoers, however, and nine would be shocked to learn that Lee did not come right out of the Brooklyn ghetto in his film *Do the Right Thing*.

If we are to be intellectually honest and promote true social equity, conscientious Americans must recognize that black racism carries the same malevolence as white racism—and act accordingly through honest identification and condemnation of black racists. It's that simple.

In June of 1964, Senator Robert Byrd (D-WV), who at the time was a recruiter for the Ku Klux Klan, led the Democrat Party's fifty-seven-day filibuster against the 1964 Civil Rights Act. It was the Republican leadership that finally stepped in and tasked Democrats to end the filibuster and accept legal equality for blacks.

Yet blacks and many other Americans elected as president a man (in President Obama) who was comfortable sitting on the same side of the aisle in the U.S. Senate as Byrd, and with membership in the party that would have kept blacks using separate rest rooms, lunch counters, and water fountains.

Consummate hypocrites among black Americans routinely heap the foulest invective upon blacks who do not buy into the mindless cult of victimization, seeing ghosts of bigoted oppressors darting at them from every corner: "Happy Negroes," "Uncle Toms," and "house niggers" are among the mildest criticisms we face on a daily basis. What's incomprehensible is that they cannot begin to fathom that it is *they* who serve in these capacities for their white Marxist overseers.

The affinity that blacks had for Barack Obama when they cast their votes for him in November 2008 was abject racism. In most cases, it wasn't the anti-white racism that was evidenced in the above correspondence, or by the old Black Panther Party, but it was racism nonetheless. History and voting trends left no doubt that black voters voted for Obama because he was black; other reasons were largely pretext.

While I'm sure it was gratifying to millions of Americans that we had come so far (in our willingness to elect a black man as president), what is overlooked is that the phenomenon of voting for him because he was black—despite the race of the voter—was itself racism. Forget the disaster that his administration promises to be for our nation. It was just as much racism as any American who voted *against* Obama because he was black.

When Obama was declared the victor in the presidential race, Rev. Jesse Jackson was seen among the thousands gathered for the election returns in Chicago, tears streaming down his face. *One of ours has finally made it,* I suppose the message was. I say "message" as opposed to the impression on Jackson's part because I doubted his sincerity. After all, this is the same man who inadvertently said that he wanted to castrate Obama on national television mere weeks before. If Jackson's goal was the parity and equality of which Martin Luther King Jr. spoke, and the Christian brotherhood toward which one would expect a reverend to strive, then what is so significant about "one of ours" having "made it"? The significance to me is that racism among black Americans is yet another misplaced entitlement.

Thanks to negrophilia and the far left, American blacks have become *more* racist since the late sixties, rather than less. If a black individual marries outside of their ethnic group (and particularly if the spouse is white), many blacks will accuse that person of having race or identity "issues." This wasn't always the case; it is a direct result of schools of thought that were promoted during and after the Civil Rights Movement by far-left whites and Afrocentric blacks. Prior to that time, there were *some* blacks who frowned upon interracial unions, but not as many as today. In many ways, blacks are more distrustful of whites now than when they had a legitimate reason to be.

In black communities, light-skinned blacks are often ridiculed for their evidencing the presence of "white blood" (although this seldom precludes darker-skinned blacks seeking them out as mates). This is a fairly recent development; in pre–Civil Rights Movement days, blacks were blacks, and their common suffrage was clear: Whites had the upper hand, no matter how light or dark a black man or woman was perceived to be by their fellows.

Causally, we have already covered the reason back of these views: The industry of civil-rights activism strives to keep the perception of oppression in the minds of black Americans. Blacks who do not buy into the propaganda have long noted that today, many black Americans spend more time in angry anti-white rhetoric and activism than they did in 1965.

Plainly put, the notion is immoral, not to mention dangerous, that achieving parity for black Americans ought to include acceptance of racism on the part of blacks. We've already seen the fruits of this acceptance, but like all of the failed and destructive devices of the far left, don't hold your breath waiting for them to admit that this was a bad idea.

AFROCENTRICITY

There is no negative connotation attached to the word "Afrocentric." The word *ought* to have a negative connotation attached to it, inasmuch as the word "ethnocentric" does, but negrophilia dictates that it be excused and accepted.

Ethnocentricity takes ethnic pride to a malignant extreme, wherein the perception of one's race is exalted above others. This can take various forms, but usually manifests in a belief in superiority of worldview, or inordinate attention toward implementation of a particular ethnic group's worldview.

Ethnocentricity—and therefore Afrocentricity—are mild forms of racism. In the perception of American blacks and many whites, however, it is yet another undesirable principle to which blacks are entitled, should they wish to subscribe to it. Whites and non-black ethnic minorities are generally not intimidated by blacks' affinity for Afrocentricity. Backed by the validation of activists, the press, and (in some cases) profiteers, the queer notion that black Americans need somehow be culturally infused with aspects of an African worldview is more or less customary.

Why?

It depends upon whom you ask. Rev. Jeremiah Wright repeated many times in his sermons, as well as in the creed of Trinity United Church, that black Americans are "an African people." Here, Rev. Wright's motivation should be obvious: He gains his livelihood by fomenting division. His premise is profoundly absurd, of course: Most black Americans are less familiar with Africa than I am with ancient Siam. The notion that they ought to have a strong affinity for, or allegiance to, things African due to the superficial verity of their genetic heritage is preposterous. How is such an outlook going to help black

Americans in any way? Arguments for this are always rooted in sentiment and narcissistic indulgence. Africans generally do not share a sense of solidarity with black Americans; on the contrary, black Africans tend to look down on black Americans as mongrelized and culturally backslidden—this is when they're not envying them for their opportunities.

The motivation for progressive Americans as to why Afrocentricity is valid varies. Some have bought into the rubbish detailed in the preceding paragraph; however, for the dedicated leftist, promoting this division is part of a political objective. If black Americans are thinking of themselves primarily as Afrocentric black née-African people, they're not thinking of themselves as Americans, are they? This holds true for every other subdivision the left has been able to identify or concoct.

> *I can't ever do it as good as a black man.*
> —GUITARIST ERIC CLAPTON, on playing the blues

It is negrophilia that leads to a rationale that spawns statements like the above. Why can't Clapton play the blues as good as a black man? *Because one simply cannot compare the suffering of a white man to that of a black man.* This is ridiculous. While it is evident that a white man cannot *relate* to the suffering of a black man who has been victimized or oppressed because of his race, it is simply not a cogent line of reasoning that a white man is incapable of experiencing a level of mental or emotional anguish sufficient to make him a good blues player. For the record, this is coming from a musician (yours truly) who can play blues.

"AFRICAN-AMERICAN"

I find the term "African-American" singularly irksome. If one peruses any one of a dozen research sources for the definition and origins of the term, the sugary-sweet, politically correct drivel to which one will be exposed just might result in a diabetic coma.

Long before the term "African-American" came into common use, it was my observation that people who identified heavily with ethnic labels (i.e., "hyphenated Americans") tended to be among the most xenophobic and bigoted. There are multitudinous ethnic groups in New York, so there was more than ample opportunity to make these observations in my youth. Americans who did not place much emphasis on their ethnicity typically used words such as "white," "black," and "Spanish" (for Latinos, despite not actually being of direct Spanish descent). Americans of Italian or Polish descent generally do not refer to themselves as "Italian-Americans" or "Polish-Americans." If asked, they'll say "Italian" or "Polish," respectively. Obviously, there are lots of Americans who are of sufficiently mixed lineage that they dispense with ethnic referents entirely. It is *progressives* that are preoccupied with the hyphen, particularly those in high-profile professions (like the press, and politicians).

Hence, when I heard it suggested that the idiom "African-American" be adopted, I thought it an extraordinarily bad idea right from the start.

The term "African-American" was actually the brainchild of a group of intellectual progressive black activists in Westchester County, New York. I was living there at the time (it was the mid-1980s), and recall reading one of the first newspaper articles wherein this think tank proposed a new name, which followed the pattern as that of other "hyphenated Americans."

In other words, the effort was completely pretentious, as well as helping to promote the exclusionary worldview that progressives have ostensibly sought to eradicate. At a time when Americans should have been striving to do away with labels, these fools maintained that we needed a *new* one. High-profile black leaders promoted use of the new term, thus sanctioning and bringing it into common use.

The sage parties who devised this apparently didn't stop to think that there was actually a difference between what was commonly understood as "black" (once "negro" or "colored") and the literal "African-American." I've heard countless instances of West Indians being referred to as African-Americans when many native West Indians are actually subjects of the British Crown or citizens of other European protectorates in the Caribbean; in other words, they're not Americans at all. President Obama—assuming he is a citizen of the U.S.—would be a true "African-American;" his father was African, and his mother, American.

Some who come upon my columns initially wonder how it is that I "get away with" saying so many things that some consider racist. Upon recognizing me as black (or of mixed race), they have their answer. Unfortunately, the truth or falsehood of such things is perceived as being predicated upon the race of the source. Much of the mail I get is from whites *and* blacks who are gratified to have found a person of color who says the things they feel they cannot say.

There's an unspoken convention that one has to be left of center to have any comprehension of the American "black experience." I was having a conversation with a relative who lives in New York about a childhood friend of ours who had become a *very* big wig at AOL Black Voices ("Black News for the African-American Community"). Being a mega-corporate interest, the Web site is of the highest quality technically; it is also very much establishment media, thus very left of center, with a decidedly VH-1/MTV feel to it. No one there would deny that "Afrocentricity" (a concept I've maintained is dangerous to start with) is the main concern. Black Voices lauds the escapades of individuals such as up-and-coming black senators, hip-hop moguls (such as Russell Simmons), is replete with scantily clad black vixens, and generally spoon-feeds black Americans urbanized, progressive, entertainment industry ideals.

To oppose AOL's right to promote Black Voices would be absurd and immoral. Also immoral, in my view, would be the failure to point out that urbanized, progressive, entertainment industry ideals are extraordinarily destructive. It's admirable that Russell Simmons is using some of his wealth to teach black South Africans how to cut diamonds, which has the potential to significantly increase their share of that nation's economy; my complaint is that Simmons made his money selling spirit poison to young black Americans in order to attain that wealth. Negrophilia gives him license to do this, whereas a white entrepreneur doing the same thing might come under scrutiny—as well he should.

And that's the crux of it: Whether one is discussing blacks or another ethnic minority in America, it's the propagandists and profiteers in the social-activist arena who won't let us simply be Americans. If confronted, they reflexively deflect blame for this deficiency toward whites. Depriving blacks of their Afrocentricity is in itself racist, don'tcha know—which leaves anyone who desires to intelligently discuss the matter between sharp pointy rocks and a hard place. "White America don't want us to have our cultcha." I've publicly scrutinized this refrain before. Why is it that only the baser and more hedonistic aspects of this "cultcha" are always the ones being defended? What about the spirituality, and the social and moral conservatism blacks embraced before the Democratic Party, infiltrated by the political left, switched gears, corrupted the black clergy, and began to enslave blacks through dependence rather than segregation and intimidation? What about blacks' ability to maintain their dignity and develop a thriving subculture during the age of segregation? What about the moral character it took to forgive and try to work with their former oppressors?

Trying to explain how such vehicles are self-serving and divisive over shouts of "racist!" and "race traitor!" is next to impossible. Sadly, the nature of blacks' sociopolitical awakening is that it will have to come in its own time—if it comes at all.

One blessing, ironically enough, is the Internet and the general expansion of informational venues in media. No doubt this has aided in the proliferation of black conservatism in recent years. While Black Voices and the like indeed have a significant effect on black Americans, there are also places a young black person can explore and come away with the realization that progressivism in America has morphed into international socialism, that the Democratic Party was the party of slavery, that it was the Democratic Party that tried to vote down the Civil Rights Act of 1964, and that Abraham Lincoln, Martin Luther King, and Johnny Ramone were Republicans.

I know: Johnny Ramone was *white*. I was just checking . . .

DYNAMICS OF INTERACTION WITH OTHER ETHNIC MINORITIES

An entire book could be written on the topic of the interaction of black Americans with other minority ethnic groups. Here, I will include a few of the more noteworthy, and perhaps newsworthy. These I have chosen because they beg elucidation, or are generally well-known but poorly understood, or because they have simply been grossly misrepresented, inadvertently or by design.

BLACKS AND JEWS

When you get right down to it, I just don't believe that civil-rights activist Rev. Jesse Jackson is all that bright. In a 1984 conversation with a *Washington Post* reporter, Jackson referred to Jews as "hymies" (an epithet that refers to Jews) and to New York City as "Hymietown" (in which Jewish people have amassed substantial political power). Initially, Jackson denied having made the remarks (don't you just *love* it when public figures deny things they've said and done that are easily verifiable?), charging Jews with conspiring to smear him. That was nearly as brilliant as having made the comments to start with. Later, he did admit to having made the remarks, and that it had been wrong, but he has made many, many profoundly scathing remarks against Jewish people over the years, never apologizing for any except the one for which he was criticized.

The fact is that with the exception of evangelical Christians, American Jews are an ethnic group that stood shoulder-to-shoulder with blacks, in the cause of civil rights, more than any other. This renders Jackson's remarks (and one would assume, his attitudes) not only racist, but rude and stupid.

Why was the reverend allowed to make such comments and retain any measure of credibility? Why was he not run out of town on a rail?

The answer lies in large letters on the cover of this book . . .

BLACKS AND ITALIANS

Here, I refer to blacks and Americans of Italian descent. Italians in Italy have a very different take on black Americans than do Americans of Italian descent, particularly in large urban areas like New York and Chicago, for example. In Italy, black Americans are associated with pop stars and sports legends as well as the numerous American athletes who regularly tour Europe, or are recruited to play on European sports teams.

The relationship between black Americans and Americans of Italian descent ("Italian-Americans") is an entirely different animal. The majority of Italian emigration to the United States took place between 1890 and 1914; almost three million came between 1900 and 1914 alone. While many had been farmers, most wound up in overcrowded tenements.

Italians were the first large wave of immigrants to the U.S. who did not speak English as a native or secondary language. Additionally, their culture was southern European, which is substantially different from that of previous immigrants such as Scandinavians, Irish, and Germans. Many were looked down upon and ostracized, being called such things as *wops, guineas, dagos,* and even *spics.* During World War II, some were even interned in camps, like many Americans of Japanese descent, although on a much smaller scale. Things did not change significantly for them until their children began to assimilate, and remaining in crowded urban areas facilitated the establishment of long-standing ethnic enclaves, and served to make many of them clannish and xenophobic themselves.

There was one ethnic group "on the block" that was universally viewed as lower on the totem pole than Italians, however. Black Americans, equally segregated, but not by choice, occupied that unenviable position. As this homegrown bigotry appeared to be part of the "American Way," Italians adopted it, disdained though they may have been by some of the Northern European–descended majority. Similar divisions had existed in Italy for centuries (such as between northern Italians and Sicilians, for example)—this was simply a more pronounced one.

This distinction needs to be made, for the dynamic is very differ-ent from that which once existed between blacks and the oppres-sive white majority. When Al Sharpton was starting out in New York, getting all the face time he could, and calling protests, most of the bigotry to which he was calling attention was not being (allegedly) perpetrated by people who represented the worldview of the majority of Americans, white or otherwise. The worldview of ethnic minorities who remain largely cloistered in ethnic neighborhoods within urban centers is unique, and differs widely from that of most Americans.

In addition, some of the enmity between blacks and Italians at that time was being generated by Sharpton himself. Sharpton asserted that blacks should have been able to frequent any neighborhood in New York City without fear for their safety. In theory, this rationale makes sense, and one might say the same for an American of Italian descent adventuring in Harlem. One could also argue that a woman ought to be able to jog in Central Park with no pants on, and not worry about being sexually assaulted.

In practice, this reasoning is imprudent at best, and insane at worst; there are some things that just aren't done. A black individual cannot strut jauntily down to Little Italy and "show his ass" (as some blacks might say, this referring to being obnoxious for obnoxiousness's sake) without expecting trouble. This agitation of the Italian community in New York was essentially tantamount to this, and simply a convenient springboard to fame for Sharpton. It didn't characterize relations between whites and blacks in America, or even between blacks and Italians. It more accurately characterized the relationship between bigoted Italians and bigoted blacks in New York.

BLACKS AND KOREANS

In March of 1991, television news viewers were treated to a highly distressing piece of video footage covering an event that had taken place in South Los Angeles on March 16. This showed a middle-aged female Asian liquor store clerk in a half-crouch behind the store's counter. In what appeared to be a braced shooter's stance, leaning next to the cash register with pistol in hand, the store owner shot a teenaged black girl as she was walking away from the counter. The girl dropped like a stone, dead.

At first blush, one cannot imagine what could possibly have prompted, or could excuse such action. The girl, fifteen-year-old Latasha Harlins, clearly had her back to the store owner. The actions of the clerk (fifty-one-year-old Soon Ja Du, a Korean immigrant who was actually a co-owner of the store) seemed almost casual. Du was subsequently convicted of voluntary manslaughter and sentenced to five years probation, which—to someone unfamiliar with the rest of the story—appeared extremely lenient.

The rest of the story was as follows: Du had caught Harlins stealing from her store. When the store owner attempted to recover the stolen item, the girl savagely assaulted the diminutive Korean. Reeling, and on the edge of insensibility, Du managed to retrieve the pistol her husband kept for defense of the store and shot Harlins in the back of the head as she retreated.

The aforementioned video footage, shown in its entirety, included Harlins repeatedly bashing Du in the head with her fist—but the footage *was not* shown in its entirety by the news bureaus that ran it. The "casual" comportment of the Korean, seen in context, was clearly one of an individual who had just had their lights nearly punched out. The fact that she had been able to get that good a shot off, having just had her head reverberated between Harlins' fist and the cash register—was actually pretty remarkable. This is, no doubt, also why Du's sentence had been so light.

Possessing an adequate background regarding the dynamics of the situation, it is not surprising at all that the situation played out as it did. People from South Korea, as a notably industrious minority that has emigrated to the United States over the last forty years or so, often start businesses that have a statistically high rate of success. Liquor stores and other high-traffic retail outlets in black neighborhoods are definitely on that list. They wouldn't be the first among successful entrepreneurs who would note that there isn't a liquor store in a given area, put one there, and clean up.

Blacks, on the other hand, who have been conditioned to learned helplessness and entitlement programs, have taken exception to "those Koreans" who move into their neighborhoods and "exploit" them. Black activists have either supported this position, or enroll blacks into resentments in neighborhoods in which there is no existing hostility. In the world in which so many urban blacks live, working for a living—let alone starting a business such as a liquor store—is either seen as being out of their reach, or too "mainstream" or middle class (something proponents of Black Liberation Theology preach, by the way). Urban black youth, such as Latasha Harlins, are educated in substandard schools, advised by activists and politicians that there is little hope for their success, and indoctrinated into the culture of self-indulgence, self-pity, and anger.

Thus, it isn't too surprising that they perceive industrious immigrants—as opposed to other similarly indoctrinated minorities—as a threat. Their position and their beliefs are racist, but in the negrophiliac paradigm, this racism is accepted because so many urban blacks remain in such a wretched state. The causes and conditions are ignored, and the symptoms overplayed, because keeping them in squalor and wretchedness is instrumental to the designs of the people who are keeping them there.

Black racism is, as many a reader may be aware, perpetuated by those political and social factions with which many politically active and socially conscious black Americans have aligned themselves. The reason why black Americans (and other minority groups) hold allegiance to the far left and the Democratic Party is a burning question among many Americans, particularly due to the latter's history of racism and oppression. I have been queried as to this phenomenon countless times. A question that has loomed large in the political arena in recent years, and chiefly among Republicans and black Republicans, is what that party might do in order to court blacks.

I realize that no matter what is said here, I am going to be considered a Republican hack by some. Most who read this book will realize that this is rubbish. Despite my believing that any resurgence of traditionalism and conservatism is likely to come from within the GOP,

I submit that the Republican Party leadership definitely deserves to have the soles of their feet beaten for the abysmal leadership they provided when they had the White House and a congressional majority. But historically, and for the last forty years in particular, the Democratic Party has done nothing but sabotage black Americans, their communities, and their institutions on every level.

That said, an analogy I have developed for elucidation is thus, given the parental nature our government insists upon taking toward Americans, and which too many of us allow: Although in a large measure the Republican and Democratic parties have grown dangerously close in terms of progressive ideology, toward the end of the Civil Rights Movement era the two parties took on the roles—as far as black Americans were concerned—of feuding, estranged parents. The Republicans were like the demonstrative, assiduous parent, who had proved their dedication and presumed that no words were needed. *Do as I say and you'll get along fine*, was their message. They were the disciplinarian, though libertarian in their practice; they weren't going to force the "child" to do anything they weren't inclined to do.

The Democrats were as the lenient, indulgent parent. Plying the "child" with goodies to win their affection, they also realized that this would give them power over their opposition—the other parent. Anything the kid demanded, they delivered, and were always quick to come up with their own ideas of what that kid might like. Whatever the kid wanted to do, they let him do it. All the while, the "tolerant" parent demonized the other, warping the child's perception of them and their motives. As a result, the offspring gravitated toward the indulgent parent, capitalized on the multitudinous offers of bequests, and resented the "strict" parent—although they still attempted to play on their sympathetic nature from time to time.

As a result, this hypothetical offspring grew up to be spoiled, arrogant, lazy, and incompetent, with a feeling of entitlement. They behaved antisocially, and found it nearly impossible to succeed within the merit-based paradigm of society. The only company in which they felt comfortable were their siblings or other spoiled, resentful brats like themselves.

Eventually, their behavior landed them in the penitentiary. Once there, of course, their resentment and anger intensified. However, they were content—such as it was—to spend visiting days sitting around with the indulgent parent, bemoaning their lot in life, and blaming their misfortunes on "maltreatment" by the industrious, authoritarian parent. The indulgent parent, of course, sympathized completely.

And so it goes . . .

So, this remains an extremely difficult question: How can Republicans (or, more aptly these days, conservatives and libertarian types) attract black Americans when the opposition plays to their baser instincts, agrees with everything they say, gives them everything they want (even though it's no good for them), and manages to successfully lay the blame for all failure on Republicans and conservatives when everything backfires? How do you compete with that?

The answer, I believe, is several-fold: A major undertaking will be the reformation of the Republican Party, which is currently dominated by elite progressive-leaning milquetoasts with less conviction than even their far-left counterparts. Unless a third party emerges that is so appealing as to appropriate nearly all conservative and many independent moderate Americans away from the Republicans, the likelihood is that any move away from the left in America will be initiated from within the Republican Party.

Those Republicans who still believe in the Republic and the Constitution are only now beginning to realize that the promise of prosperity, self-esteem, and security has paled in the eyes of black Americans compared to the false promise of socialist redistribution of whitey's wealth to them.

In order to convey their message, Republicans and conservatives, though it might be contrary to their nature, are going to have to become similarly ruthless and duplicitous in their modus operandi in order to counter the treachery and absence of restraint on the part of their opposition. The "bigger gun" theory always works, contrary to what progressives preach. It will obviously never do to assume that blacks know which party stood against slavery and segregation, any more than it will do to assume that most Americans know that less taxes and less spending promote economic growth, and that more taxes and more spending stultify economic growth.

In order to accomplish this, advancing those social, political, and (limited) government institutions that will actually aid in helping black Americans to thrive must also commence, as must the weakening of those which do not. The National Education Association (NEA), for example, ought to be systematically infiltrated by more conservative and libertarian-minded people, if not abolished altogether. Young conservatives must be encouraged to enter fields currently dominated by those in the far left, such as the press, and systematic designs for their insinuation into these careers must be devised.

Those politicians and prominent activists who conspire to keep blacks in ignorance and dependency must be revealed for what they are. Ruthless measures, such as counterintelligence programs, should be initiated. Prominent far-left operatives and professional civil-rights activists routinely come under scrutiny for nefarious dealings; many more might be revealed if focused efforts were being made to root them out. The stock of these parasites in the eyes of Americans (and black Americans in particular) would plummet if only conscientious Americans of influence capitalized on such occurrences.

Even given this plan of action, it could still take generations before the number of blacks who mainstream and succeed working within the framework of society (assuming American society remains intact for that long) eclipses that of those who remain ensconced within the camp of the far left—replete with its misery and failure. The sad fact is that the majority of black Americans are poised to follow the far left dedicatedly into the fires of hell and then blame the temperature on faceless white oppressors.

Finally, the gravest immediate threat to Americans at large (vis-à-vis black racism) lies in the nihilistic black power brokers who are now at the height of their influence; whether they augment this power remains to be seen. I am referring to those of extreme black national-istic sentiments who have insinuated themselves into influential posi-tions. Examples of these are Harvard professors Henry Louis Gates Jr. and Charles Ogletree, and, of course, President Obama.

For individuals such as these, merely succeeding within the system, "getting their due," as it were, is not enough. They are so deeply hate-ful of whites and this nation that they reside in that moment of time—during the Civil Rights Movement—in which tearing "the system" down was the favored goal. Despite having become prominent and, in many cases, quite wealthy, they are literally willing to destroy every existing social and political institution in America. Some of these are younger blacks who have bought into the "racist America" worldview, but most are older individuals who have been crafting their designs (along with white progressives and many Marxists) since the 1960s. They envision securing the "absolute power" they believe that the soul-less white racists once held, and wielding it every bit as ruthlessly and cruelly. Despite the strides in racial equality in America, their hatred of whites runs too deep. Like General Zod from the 1970s *Superman* films, though their oppressors may be long dead, they apparently feel that they will be vindicated if they can make those oppressors' descen-dants "pay."

Surviving the process and its aftermath is of no concern to them; in their narcissistic view—which is quite characteristic of those on the far left—they will be princes in the new order. At this point, they have no reason not to believe it, either. Just look at how far Obama has risen.

Unlike activists such as Jesse Jackson, these men (and a few women) are the true backbone of black progressive power in America; they are arguably more dangerous than billionaire financier George Soros or the American Civil Liberties Union (ACLU) at this juncture, because they have exacted a significant toll on our social relations, Americans' worldview, and (as will be covered later) the American economy.

In the event that you're ready to fashion a tinfoil hat for me, I would add that much of the methods, if not the motives I offer here, have been widely documented.

Where are the oppressors against whom these men rail? The little white men in suits and fedoras we can see in black-and-white newsreels and documentary footage who upheld segregation and Jim Crow, fearful of their women being carried off by horny black bucks, are gone. That brand of racist no longer has any power in America. The only white racists I see are lying in bed beside these black professors, activists, and politicians—and they have big, satisfied smiles on their faces.

NINE

the media—
spreading the ailment

O NCE AGAIN, "BLACKS in the American Media" might merit another entire tome, given the anecdotal evidence and dynamics connected to the subject. Here, brevity will have to serve to get the message across.

THE ENTERTAINMENT INDUSTRY

In 1971, veteran television producer Norman Lear premiered a situation comedy called *All in the Family*. It featured patriarch Archie Bunker, a caricature of the white bigot. He was an urban New York working-class guy—and he was an idiot. His only redeeming qualities were his work ethic and loyalty to his family. Present-day reference sources, of course, refer to him as "conservative," but he wasn't intelligent enough to even define the term. Most of the laughs in the show were derived from Archie's bigotry, the derision of Archie's bigotry, as well as the ongoing tête-à-tête between him and his liberal son-in-law, Mike. The latter was intelligent, educated, open-minded, and quick with a comeback.

I would note here that Archie Bunker did not faithfully represent the majority of his demographic in any way.

The show wound up being one of the biggest hits of all time. As a result, many of the stereotypes—both positive and negative—represented therein became part of the American collective consciousness and the developing zeitgeist.

One of Archie's nemeses in *All in the Family* was George Jefferson. George and his wife Louise were Archie and Edith Bunker's neighbors. They were black and fairly well-off. George Jefferson was every bit the bigot Archie was; yet there was never an indication given that there was anything wrong with this; in fact, it was glossed over so smoothly as to be a non-issue. It was George's entitlement, you see, restitution for George's portion of suffering on the part of all blacks. The Jeffersons' popularity resulted in a spin-off series of the same name. While it wasn't as big a hit as *All in the Family*, it was quite successful, becoming nearly as iconic. Hence, the subliminal messages of these ventures did their part to advance negrophilia, as well as to validate black racism.

These programs are but examples of what was transpiring on a more widespread basis at the time. Whether they reflected the beliefs of those involved in their production, or were Lear's perception of his contribution to "the cause" (Lear also founded the far-left political group People for the American Way in 1981), is anyone's guess. Similar fare that did not enjoy the success of *All in the Family* or *The Jeffersons* saturated the airwaves and celluloid media.

Mandingo was a 1975 film adapted from the book of the same name (authored by Kyle Onstott). It starred legendary actor James Mason, boxer Ken Norton, and Perry King, whose promising career I believe suffered immensely as a result of his full frontal nudity in the film. Although it wasn't a huge success (partly due to its graphic nature), it went a long way to solidifying the image of slave owners as Neanderthals. Granted that many of the events therein were faithfully fictionalized representations of things that occurred in the antebellum South—but the characterizations were atrocious. The Maxwell family (around whom the story was centered) and their contemporaries were so dim it was difficult to believe they could walk and keep their hearts beating at the same time. Their white associates and those in their employ were even worse. The patriarch (played by James Mason) spoke with a knock-off Foghorn Leghorn accent that threatened to leave the viewer with terminal laugh-face.

This representation belied the fact that (while I'm not out to glorify slave owners) people of the social station represented by the Maxwells were often fabulously wealthy, educated their children abroad, spoke numerous languages, and were not much different from well-heeled people from any other society during that period.

While *All in the Family* and *The Jeffersons* were calculated to demonize white bigots and inculcate the idea that black bigotry was acceptable, respectively, *Mandingo,* rather than simply demonizing slave owners, demonized whites and Southerners in general, reinforcing the stereotype of the uncool, rhythmless, oblivious white buffoon that was being portrayed in more contemporary productions. It also added to the myth of black sexual prowess; one of the subplots depicted the younger Maxwell's wife (played by Susan George) satisfying that which she could not seem to satisfy within her marriage, with Norton's character, the strapping black slave, wink-wink, nudge-nudge.

This fare had the potential to make great cinema while telling a story and relating the evils of slavery, but films such as *Mandingo* wound up being blatantly propagandistic and as ridiculous as *Blacula.* These are just a few poignant examples of thousands of instances of negrophilia within hundreds of television programs and films produced over the last few decades.

Not all manifestations of negrophilia are grave and potentially harmful; some are simply inane and unfortunate. Countless insidious little examples, the result of incessant subliminal conditioning, occur during the course of any given day. One needs only to look.

For example: Actor Ben Kingsley won the Academy Award for his work in the 1982 film *Gandhi*, in which he portrayed legendary Indian civil-rights activist Mohandas K. Gandhi. That year, Kingsley was up against American actor Dustin Hoffman for his portrayal of Michael Dorsey, a down-and-out actor who gained work and fame when he decided to interview for a role as a woman, Dorothy Michaels.

Both Hoffman and Kingsley did masterful jobs, but one cannot say that either outshone the other. *I* would say that Dustin Hoffman playing a woman is much more of a theatrical stretch than Ben Kingsley (who was born Krishna Pandit Bhanji in 1943) playing an Indian. *I* would submit that the Academy of Motion Picture Arts and Sciences, a decidedly progressive entity, deemed that bestowing the Best Actor award upon a little brown man that year superseded any notions of groundbreaking thespian achievement.

THE RECORDING INDUSTRY

It is amazing (in a profoundly sad way) that animated, shrill, vociferous activists in the vein of President Obama's former "energy czar" Van Jones (who resigned in September 2009 after video footage surfaced that included Jones making profane, racist comments and advancing summary redistribution of economic resources) routinely accuse shadowy white forces of such outrageous, nebulous charges as poisoning black communities and stacking the criminal justice system against blacks, yet every fad or popular trend that is harmful to blacks is defended by the same parties *in the name of blackness.*

One of the worst offenders, and one of the cultural icons most ardently defended of late, has been rap music. I've already detailed the specifics regarding this cultural phenomenon and its negative message. Certainly, the entertainment media (television, films, and music) have received indictments across the board as behaving irresponsibly as regards the sorts of messages they impart to the public, particularly American youth.

I could paint a conspiratorial picture of the phenomenon of the recording industry seeking to debase black Americans to the end of keeping them in a socially wretched condition, but that would be dishonest; doing so in order for it to fit within a favored paradigm would make me no better than a Van Jones. I believe that those who profit via the marketing of rap, rap artists, and other socially questionable media do so because it makes money. It makes money because it is easy to market. It's easy to market because these lifestyles play to people's baser nature; self-indulgence has a great and primal, titillating appeal. The lack of responsibility of record moguls is no different than that of contractors in the building industry who employ the use of shabby materials. It's a cheap and easy route to wealth.

It is apparent, however, that the ancillary social engineering aspect of the recording industry's effect on black youth has increased since the 1980s. The reason for this may be a function of the advent of music videos, which offered a more comprehensive picture of the trendy lifestyles being purveyed, whether rock, the dance club culture, hip-hop, or gangsta rap.

Once again, the manner in which this fits into the scope of this book is in the lack of acknowledgment of the harm being done. The few commentators and social activists who have criticized the recording industry for its part in subverting black youth have been excoriated as racists (or race traitors) and denigrated for attempting, once more, to deny black people their various freedoms. For those who choose to point these things out, other than the knowledge of having served their conscience, it's a lose-lose proposition.

THE PRESS

One has to realize that inasmuch as all areas of media have advanced progressives and their designs, negrophilia and its auxiliary features have been dedicatedly promoted as well. As far as representations of blacks in the news media go, on the national level, the conventional wisdom has been as follows: America is still, largely, a racist nation, and blacks are still institutionally oppressed. Black Americans who become successful by simply capitalizing on the opportunities that became available to them since the civil rights movement are generally ignored if they happen to be overtly traditional, conservative, or apolitical. To be fair, this is excepting those who have excelled in mass market exploits, such as sports and entertainment.

Who are held up as examples of success? Those who have taken up the cause of far-left and/or black activism. Those who snipe about America being institutionally racist and imperialist, and who tend to support favored far-left causes. This includes, but is not limited to, career activists, activist professors (Harvard professor Henry Louis Gates Jr. is counted as one of the most prominent), and entertainers in the far-left camp, as well as the crop of abysmally ignorant, young black music artists who know nothing about the history of the United States or even the civil rights movement, yet never miss a chance to prattle on about America being a racist nation the moment they see a camera in front of them.

A stellar example of this is rapper Kanye West, who received national attention for his excoriation of President Bush following Hurricane Katrina in 2005. West blathered the most intellectually retarded, baseless accusations vis-à-vis the Bush administration's handling (or mishandling) of evacuation and relief efforts. There wasn't even a concern among news agencies that this uninformed young man might make himself look bad; he was paid all the deference of an individual with PhDs in civil engineering and meteorology. Part of this phenomenon is due to the industry-fostered adulation of celebrities; they generally possess such little wisdom that I wouldn't trust them to recommend a burger joint, but credence is given to them when they happen to be black, and commenting on an issue of race.

Conversely, when prominent blacks lean a micrometer right of center, or if they *step out of their place* and attempt to deliver a traditional or conservative message, they are harshly criticized. This was the case when Bill Cosby collectively spanked the black community back in 2004.

Clarence Thomas was nominated for the position of Supreme Court justice in 1991 by President George H.W. Bush to succeed Justice Thurgood Marshall. As a conservative black man, he was dragged across miles of salted, rusty razor blades—naked—during his confirmation hearings by congressional Democrats and the press. It is worth noting that the only fundamental difference between Thomas and Sonia Sotomayor, nominated eighteen years later, is their politics and the fact that the latter actually exhibited rulings and beliefs that ought to have exempted her from serving on the Court.

This aforementioned razor-blade dragging was all acceptable, you see, in the eyes of the press, and their coverage reflected it. Thomas, as a conservative, was not *minding his place.* He was not one of the bellowing, accusatory activist set. He had not made his way along the career path via affirmative action. As such, he was a house nigger at best, an Uncle Tom at worst. Thus, he was fair game. Against a dominant and complicit press, who was there to report the injustice of his public scourging?

The O.J. Simpson trial was negrophilia at its finest. For any who have been living off-planet for the last twenty years, Orenthal James "O. J." Simpson (nicknamed "The Juice") was a legendary black football hero turned actor and corporate spokesman. He'd come up in the sixties, when the success of a black man, particularly to the degree he succeeded, really meant something.

On June 12, 1994, Simpson's estranged second wife, Nicole Brown, and a male friend were found gruesomely murdered outside Brown's home. An edged device was used so liberally that a witness to the aftermath described "a river of blood" on the walkway, and Brown's head had been nearly severed. Inasmuch as the evidence strongly suggested Simpson was the killer, he was charged with their murders and put on trial.

Part of the reason race became such an issue here was due to the fact that this all came in the wake of the Los Angeles riots of 1992. The riots had been the result of the acquittal of three police officers for the beating of Rodney King, a black man. On March 2, 1991, King had been stopped by Los Angeles police officers for speeding. The speeding violation escalated into a drunk driving charge, which escalated into a full-on fight with the police. Whatever occurred, the incident ended with the police Tasering and then brutally beating King. It all might have gone down as another case of a drunk driver resisting arrest, had the beating not been caught on video by a private citizen from his apartment.

Given the widespread airing of the videotape by media outlets, the incident became an iconic validation of the long-held public belief that L.A. police were particularly corrupt and brutal, especially where black men were concerned. It made for an atmosphere of great tension in Southern California during the trial of the police officers charged in the beating.

The news of the acquittal gave rise to the riots. Putting the riots down ultimately involved police, the U.S. Army, Marines, and the National Guard. Fifty-three people were killed, over two thousand were injured, and there was $1 billion in financial losses. Thus, almost immediately after O.J. Simpson was arrested for the murders, there was an undercurrent of suspicion in the community and the press that this might be a biased prosecution because Simpson was black, not to mention anxiety over what might ensue were he convicted.

The fact that none of us were flies on the wall outside Nicole Brown's condo that night notwithstanding, it was pretty much a slam-dunk regarding Simpson's guilt. He was a super-aggressive male who'd had the world on a platter since he was very young, and that, as it does to many in positions of awesome celebrity, spoiled him. The Brown-Simpson marriage had been punctuated by countless incidents of domestic violence. After the couple separated, Simpson manifested stalking behavior. During the proceedings, one of the exhibits introduced was a 911 audiotape with the voice of Nicole Simpson screaming that O.J. was about to kill her. From before their marriage in 1985, Simpson treated Nicole as nothing more than his little sex trophy. He cheated on her and beat her regularly, as well as emotionally abusing her. Their circle of friends was replete with those who had been witnesses to the domestic violence over the years, and with professionals who had counseled them in this area.

When police arrived at Simpson's estate to notify him of the murders, they found a blood stain on Simpson's Ford Bronco, and more blood leading toward the house. They also found a bloody glove that matched one found at the murder scene.

As the evidence mounted, it was practically overwhelming. All of it, however, was overshadowed by the racial overtones, accusations of racism on the part of the police, and the issue Simpson's defense made of the race component. Simpson put together a cadre of mercenary attorneys ("The Dream Team," the press called them, the best his vast financial resources could buy) to defend him; some were even celebrities in their own right. They accentuated the racial elements of the case even more.

Then, during the trial, one of the detectives who had been called to the murder scene that night, Mark Fuhrman, was caught in a lie. While being questioned by the defense as to his perception of blacks during the course of his career and his treatment of them while on the job, he was asked if he had ever used the term "nigger." He said he had certainly uttered the word during his lifetime, but that he had not used it in many years. Of course, Simpson's defense team already had thirteen hours of audiotape of Fuhrman using the word "nigger" quite freely—and definitely more recently than he had indicated. Whether or not his status as a hardened racist had been established, his status as a liar certainly had.

Well, if Fuhrman had lied about that, the implication was: Might he not have been capable of planting evidence or lying about what was found that night, and where? The case pretty much fell apart right there: A racist liar from an historically racist and brutal police department who had been in a position to mishandle evidence, probably sought to frame this phenomenally successful, wealthy black man because he was black, *and* he had been married to a white woman. Indeed, there was evidence introduced into the record indicating that Fuhrman had a deep disdain for interracial couples, and would summarily pull them over when he encountered them while cruising in his department vehicle.

Part of the upshot of the Simpson trial was the viral adoption of the phrase "N-word" in place of the word "nigger" in public circles, the media in particular. "Did you ever use the N-word?" Fuhrman was asked (bear in mind that the trial took place in politically correct Los Angeles, where men who are *not* gay carry handbags and clutch purses). Over and over again, the phrase served as the alternative for "nigger" during the most-televised criminal trial in American history.

"The N-word" became part of the American lexicon from then on.

By then, in a very real sense, none of the evidence mattered. Although Simpson was later found culpable in a civil wrongful-death trial, he was acquitted in the criminal case. To this day, many take it as a given that Simpson was guilty, but beat the system due to his fame and money. In my view, I would also add *negrophilia*: The justice system performed in this perverse manner due to Simpson's race, press involvement, and the zeitgeist in action. Some people even seemed to believe that Simpson's acquittal, if in error, was still acceptable inasmuch as it could serve as partial restitution for all of the black men who'd been persecuted by police in the past, and by the LAPD in particular.

All of the aforementioned phenomena have been media-driven. As with much of their advancing of the far left's agenda, in the case of negrophilia it is no different. If anything, the entertainment media and the press have been at least as guilty (more so for the press, if one considers its ostensible mission) than politicians and activists. They grab whatever inane social engineering idea the hard left comes up with, and run with it like a starved big-game fish.

Like "Ebonics"! Now, what kind of a "definitive book on race politics in America" would this be without a discussion of Ebonics, I ask you?

"Ebonics" is a term generally considered to have been coined by Afrocentric George Washington University professor Robert Williams. Initially, his rationale was that it was impertinent for white teachers to correct black children due to their use of vernacular particular to black Americans. Other progressive and Afrocentric professors as well as California's Oakland school board got on board with this nonsense and began compiling "dictionaries" of "black vernacular." Their assertion was that this "language" ought to be considered as valid as Standard English in the classroom.

Almost immediately the establishment press began to publicize Ebonics, and the debate began, not as to whether or not this swill ought to be incorporated into the accepted lexicon, but *how* to do so.

My initial reaction was abject horror. *They're actually going to validate urban black patois?* I thought. *One of the chief causes that black people, particularly schoolchildren, have trouble succeeding?*

But I was missing the premise, of course. Far-left educators whose PhDs were printed on toilet paper, and activists, such as those who wish to bilingualize all of America, were rebelling against the very language we speak. *The white man's language.* No, they assert; everyone else must accommodate the deviation, because the status quo—European-based values and language—is manifestly evil. We must integrate and validate the very things that are stultifying minds and subverting society because *it's a black thing,* you wouldn't understand, and besides: Blacks are entitled.

The crime here is not the concept of Ebonics itself, or the fact that it was capricious, childish folly. Here, members of the press are either stupid and reckless for going along with a harmful idiocy, or they're evil, if they're engaging in something that will harm black people by design. In any case, the press has vigorously promoted every injurious social perversion that has come over the transom, more often on the implied if not explicit grounds that past history *entitles* black people to it.

I mentioned bilingualism. Negrophilia was also a precursor to the bilingual movement. Growing up in New York, I remember seeing signs in Spanish everywhere. This is not surprising for a couple of reasons: At that time, New York was on its way to having more Puerto Ricans than Puerto Rico, and New York was a bastion of progressivism.

The point I wish to make is this: The need for bilingual signs and advertising was public safety and profit motive, respectively. It was simply done out of necessity. There was no wholesale political press (at that juncture) to change American tradition or insinuate inordinate amounts of Puerto Rican culture into the American worldview. Some of this occurred, of course, but no more than was natural or inevitable due to normal exposure, as was the case with other ethnic groups that integrated into American society.

The success of negrophilia in the cultural arena facilitated the advancement of bilingualism and other alterations in the collective worldview desired by progressives; it was the "given inch" that allowed them to request, nay, demand that everything from the language to various retrograde rituals of émigrés be respectfully observed. Today, we have American Jewish progressives who advocate for the rights of Muslims to operate schools that instruct in Sharia law right here in America. This is insanity, of course; these are the first people whom radical Muslims in America would eradicate if given their druthers.

Finally, despite the laughable and repeated assertion on the part of far-left pundits that the conservative press holds inordinate sway over the worldview of the American people and is a grave threat to liberty, the truth is precisely the opposite. The only threat the conservative press poses is to the political left itself. As such, most black journalists—and certainly most prominent ones—act as operatives for the left, articulating the doctrine of victimhood, and decrying continued institutional racism.

Such luminaries as Eugene Robinson of the *Washington Post,* Clarence Page of the *Chicago Tribune,* and syndicated columnist Roland Martin articulate the party line very well, but it's still the party line. The National Association of Black Journalists (NABJ) is essentially one of dozens of precincts for the Diversity Police, a chorus of dissatisfaction and racist paranoia. One might say that these organizations (and the individuals who represent them) are more dangerous than the inarticulate street-level activists, because most *are* well-educated and articulate.

The danger to our society and black Americans lies in their perceived credibility; given the fact that they (and black professionals in other high-profile industries) have been educated in universities that have constructed well-developed black-studies departments over the last few decades that are essentially dedicated to promoting far-left and negrophiliac sensibilities, theirs is often taken as "the last word."

TEN

the legal system

ANYONE WHO FOLLOWS current events in America is aware that the rate of incarceration of blacks, young black males in particular, is inordinately high. Depending on one's source for statistical data, the estimates are that blacks account for between 35 percent to 40 percent of inmates in American prisons. Some even claim that fully half of America's 2.2 million incarcerated individuals are black.

Certain prominent activists and organizations would have us believe that the majority of these prisoners were unceremoniously plucked from America's streets for no reason, tried in kangaroo courts, and packed off to penitentiaries. At best, they hold that criminal laws in America have been written expressly to "target" blacks, thus resulting in the same outcome.

It is undeniable that profiling, police brutality, and unfair sentencing practices were factors in the legal system when America was institutionally racist, and figured largely in the treatment of black Americans who found themselves on the wrong side of the law, as it were. It is also true that there are still racist individuals in the legal system. Things are getting better for blacks economically (in the aggregate), yet more (in percentages) are going to prison. Why?

The primary factor I would introduce apropos the charge that the legal system in the U.S. is racist, or that the cards are stacked against black people therein, is this: *The incarceration rate among blacks hasn't always been this high.* In 1959 (pre-desegregation), blacks accounted for—at most—around 30 percent of those incarcerated. This is still a lot, in statistical terms, but perhaps not when you account for the fact that in 1959, this *was* an institutionally racist nation. "In historical perspective, the 910,000 African-Americans incarcerated today are more than nine times the number of 98,000 in 1954, the year of the *Brown v. Board of Education* decision."[5]

Heather MacDonald, a Manhattan Institute senior fellow and a contributing editor to its magazine, *City Journal,* penned an article for the Spring 2008 issue that presents many of the core arguments that I and like-minded colleagues usually keep in our utility belts. It was so succinct that I am compelled to include an excerpt here. In addition, since so few scholars are able and willing to declare the truth as it pertains to such sensitive issues, I believe there is a certain practicality to include supporting materials from those with credentials in specialty areas.

Ms. MacDonald's essay contains key facts toward explaining the numbers apropos black incarceration in America—not that facts matter to those who typically disagree with me, but I eschew making important statistical claims without at least some credible reference.

> The race industry and its elite enablers take it as self-evident that high black incarceration rates result from discrimination. At a presidential primary debate this Martin Luther King Day, for instance, Sen. Barack Obama charged that blacks and whites "are arrested at very different rates, are convicted at very different rates, [and] receive very different sentences . . . for the same crime. . . ."
>
> If a listener didn't know anything about crime, such charges of disparate treatment might seem plausible. After all, in 2006, blacks were 37.5% of all state and federal prisoners, though they're under 13% of the national population. About one in 33 black men was in prison in 2006, compared with one in 205 white men and one in 79

Hispanic men. Eleven percent of all black males between the ages of 20 and 34 are in prison or jail.

The dramatic rise in the correctional population over the past three decades—to 2.3 million people at the end of 2007—has only amplified the racial accusations against the criminal-justice system. The favorite culprits for high black prison rates include a biased legal system, draconian drug enforcement, and even prison itself. None of these explanations stands up to scrutiny.

The black incarceration rate is overwhelmingly a function of black crime. Insisting otherwise only worsens black alienation and further defers a real solution to the black crime problem.

Racial activists usually remain silent about that problem. But in 2005, the black homicide rate was more than seven times higher than that of whites and Hispanics combined, according to the Federal Bureau of Justice Statistics. From 1976 to 2005, blacks committed more than 52% of all murders in America. In 2006, the black arrest rate for most crimes was two to nearly three times blacks' representation in the population. Blacks constituted 39.3% of all violent-crime arrests, including 56.3% of all robbery and 34.5% of all aggravated-assault arrests, and 29.4% of all property-crime arrests.

The advocates acknowledge such crime data only indirectly: by charging bias on the part of the system's decision makers. As Obama suggested in the Martin Luther King debate, police, prosecutors, and judges treat blacks and whites differently "for the same crime."

But in fact, cops don't over-arrest blacks and ignore white criminals. The race of criminals reported by crime victims matches arrest data. No one has ever come up with a plausible argument as to why crime victims would be biased in their reports.

Unfair drug policies are an equally popular explanation for black incarceration rates. Legions of pundits, activists, and academics charge that the war on drugs is a war on minorities.

They point to federal crack penalties, the source of the greatest amount of misinformation in the race and incarceration debate.

Under a 1986 law, five grams of crack triggers a mandatory minimum five-year sentence in federal court; powder-cocaine traffickers get the same five-year minimum for 500 grams.

The media love to target the federal crack penalties because crack defendants are likely to be black. In 2006, 81% of federal crack defendants were black while only 27% of federal powder-cocaine defendants were. Since federal crack rules are more severe than those for powder, and crack offenders are disproportionately black, those rules must explain why so many blacks are in prison, the conventional wisdom holds.

But consider that in 2006, only 5,619 crack sellers were tried federally, 4,495 of them black. It's going to take a lot more than 5,000 or so crack defendants a year to account for the 562,000 black prisoners in state and federal facilities at the end of 2006—or the 858,000 black prisoners in custody overall, if one includes the population of county and city jails.

Moreover, the press almost never mentions the federal methamphetamine-trafficking penalties, which are identical to those for crack. In 2006, the 5,391 sentenced federal meth defendants were 54% white, 39% Hispanic and 2% black. No one calls the federal meth laws anti-Hispanic or anti-white.

The evidence is clear: Black prison rates result from crime, not racism. The dramatic drop in crime in the 1990s, to which stricter sentencing policies unquestionably contributed, has freed thousands of law-abiding inner-city residents from the bondage of fear.[6]

First off, one can see that there are discrepancies in the actual number of blacks being sentenced to penitentiaries among scholars and statisticians. It could be postulated that black activists are inflating the numbers for their own purposes. For the sake of argument, I will concur here that although we may not be able to nail down the precise figures, blacks account for a disproportionately high percentage of prison inmates in the U.S.

If—as I'm arguing—America is not an institutionally racist nation, and criminal laws have not been crafted to result in high incarceration rates among black Americans, then why do they account for an admittedly high percentage of inmates in America's penitentiaries?

Glad you asked.

We've examined the data affirming the increased upward mobility of black Americans, and acknowledged the increase in their incarceration rates. As you recall, I covered poverty rates among black Americans in a previous chapter. It is more than a curious incongruity that as black Americans have been succeeding in the aggregate, more of their number have been falling through the cracks—and right into penitentiaries. My hypothesis is one that reflects negrophilia and places America in a place analogous to that of the ancient Aztecs, who would take precious and revered members of their society, and brutally sacrifice them.

If you happen to be someone who has been compelled through some adversity to seek public assistance for a time—though you may have resisted tooth and nail—then you will understand the following scenarios on a visceral level.

For Americans who possess a work ethic, a sense of integrity, and, yes, even pride, the prospect of relying on public assistance (I am loath to call it "government assistance," since it isn't the government's money—it's the public's) inspires a sense of primal revulsion. What it does to one's sense of self-worth and emotional sense of well-being can be catastrophic.

Even if one is intellectually resolved to principles of Scripture, karma, or any of the other doctrines that hold to people helping one another, humility, and reciprocity, the effects of dependency have the potential to be nearly as deleterious as the misfortune that brought the person to a place of such need. It's nearly impossible to relate to someone who has not shared the experience, although there are probably many more people now who have had the experience than there were in the beginning of 2008.

Imagine then, if you will—and likely you can *only* imagine—being born into an environment in which this lifestyle was the norm. You know from an early age that you're on the bottom of the human food chain. Welfare is the topic of childhood jokes and barbs. Mom doesn't work; if there is a dad, he probably doesn't live with you, as the monetary benefits are easier to obtain and more copious for single-parent households. Still, you are aware that there is more available in the country in which you live, and kids who dress better and eat better, and whose parents are able to spoil them, if only a little or on occasion. It should go without saying that this is positively grotesque modeling for a young child.

Presume further that you're sent to substandard schools, where children from every other poor, dysfunctional home in the area are educated. The teachers are overburdened and frustrated; there are shortages of everything; there's violence, widespread conflicts of all varieties and the attendant twisted relationships. Perhaps this is combined with a particularly unpleasant home life. School performance suffers, and you begin to get messages from adults (including teachers) that your life after school doesn't hold much promise. If there's juvenile delinquency in the mix, or brushes with the law, these messages may be quite potent. All of this translates into a feeling of hopelessness—that there's no way out.

In short, *life sucks.*

And, all the while, you have an innate feeling that it's not your fault—and of course, it isn't. You were, after all, born into all this. You develop feelings of simmering anger and resentment, all the more potent contingent upon just how disagreeable your situation is in general. Many of those around you feel the same way; occasionally you hear them complain about employers at dismal jobs, rude clerks at state offices, the police, and "the Man."

You turn on the radio, and your pain is validated via the medium of gangsta rap. On the television, there's a conglomeration of stimuli—some of which you cannot identify with at all, some that's marginally entertaining, and some that's the audiovisual equivalent of what you hear on the radio. Occasionally, you see an impassioned black man standing before a microphone and a crowd of other impassioned black people, decrying "the system" that universally dooms black people to just the manner of life you live.

Over time, your perception evolves into a morass of hopelessness, anger, and resentment—convinced that somewhere, there's a greedy, avaricious, faceless white suit who is responsible for it all.

On the street, however, you see a few people who are like you, and who *do* have access to some of the wonderful things that are so coveted by people in society, both within and outside of your squalid surroundings. They're criminals, of course, but what does that matter? Isn't what is being done to you and just about everyone you know, a form of criminality? The law is a joke. Besides, these people command respect that you don't see others receiving, something you'd like to have. They're not hopeless; they're not powerless.

So what do you do? Your sense of moral obligation has become pretty grotesque, given the bizarre environment to which you've been exposed all of your life. You feel as deserving as the next guy, and you're not lazy—you're just not willing to be abused and humiliated for minimum wage, like so many people you know.

If there's a gang presence in your community, well, you've already got a handy and organized framework to fit into. You don't have to reinvent the wheel; it's practically like getting hired by a well-established corporation. These are people just like you; beyond angry, they practically worship chaos itself. There are a variety of "positions" you might fill; all that's needed is guts (or sociopathy) and the willingness to perform.

It's also a great outlet for your anger . . .

You forget about the faceless white suit; he's as unassailable as God—but there are others upon whom you can transfer your hostilities. The other "sets" (gangs), the competition; they become the enemy, and it's a fight to the death.

The culture is self-seeking; all of the primal satisfactions one can imagine, all of the sensory stimulation, are accessible aplenty: wanton sex, mind-altering substances, ego-gratification, control, danger. It is a true subculture, isolated even from most black Americans. The streets are an exciting, electric jungle, and everyone, save for your comrades-in-arms, is either a hunter to be feared, or prey to be taken.

Your existence is validated by your peers, certain members of your community, and even elements of the press. The only downside is the risk of incarceration or death—and every endeavor has its downside.

This is but one theoretical example, but I'm sure you get the point. Multiply that times all of the neighborhoods in which this is taking place, times all of the urban areas in America. The beginning of this example explained, in a nutshell, why this life followed the path that it did. *The cause* represents something that has proliferated on a grand scale since the civil-rights era: *dependency*. The dependency of black Americans on government handouts. *Entitlements*. This is the chief reason crime, and the attendant incarceration rate among blacks, has increased.

A secondary reason is the propaganda relative to the aforementioned perception of helplessness on our subject's part. It is *by design* that so many blacks in America have been poorly educated, and it is by design that they remain poorly informed, via the parties who are on the same page: politicians, self-serving activists, and the establishment press. It is a cycle: The worse conditions get (or appear), the louder the plaintive cries of activists become. This facilitates politicians declaring that they need more public resources (read *money*) in order to ameliorate these conditions—and anyone who opposes this idea is, of course, a racist. The establishment press conveniently ignores the argument routinely put forth by their opposition; this being that far-left politicians have spent billions since 1965 on social programs, yet conditions for urban black Americans (in the aggregate) have only gotten worse. So blacks at large don't even get to consider *that* train of thought.

Money strengthens the political machine, better enabling politicians to keep blacks enslaved via entitlements. Since they do nothing to address the real problems (which would naturally be self-defeating), things get worse. So the cycle continues.

An ancillary factor in this phenomenon is one that is no longer widely discussed, as it is not politically correct. It has, however, been studied, and observed by sociologists and commentators of every political persuasion. This has to do with the detrimental effects of dependency upon the psyche of men who cannot—or perceive that they cannot—provide for their families. The sense of self-worth tied to this relational dynamic is hard-wired into males, as much as feminists and feminized researchers might assert otherwise, or contend that it is an incorrect or defective perception. When a husband and father finds himself in this position, regardless of socioeconomic class, the results can be horrific. In the short term, the resulting stressors can lead to all sorts of dysfunction, including substance abuse, domestic violence, and even suicide.

In the long term? Well, this syndrome can be examined in microcosm in impoverished or distressed families of any ethnic background; however, it became an endemic aspect of the experience of blacks in America. Here, a significant portion of the male population in this ethnic subgroup was emasculated. The results of the wholesale manifestation of this syndrome within a vast segment of a population—in this case, blacks—are there for all to see.

In this area, negrophilia might be viewed as a social experiment that has worked very well. Subverting social paradigms, eradicating traditional social units and conventions (such as the family and churches), has been an increasingly useful tool for the hard left. In this example, they saw that they were able to effectively influence hearts and minds via mythologizing blacks, while still controlling and maintaining them as political allies.

Attendant to all of this was the secularization of black Americans. As stated earlier, the black clergy at large was coerced into the fold through token political power and wealth. They ceased preaching the message of God and supplanted it with the message of hopelessness and victimization. Faith had been the one thing holding black communities together through the trials and injustices they had faced. The legal obstacles were finally lifted, but blacks had now been stripped of vital spiritual leaders. Reliance upon God was forgotten; survival became a case of reliance upon the state, or upon one's own devices.

✐

On July 16, 2009, Harvard University professor Henry Louis Gates Jr. was arrested for disorderly conduct at his home after Cambridge, Massachusetts, police contacted him there, responding to a call about a possible home invasion. When queried, Gates began screaming about being profiled as a criminal because he was "a black man in America," accusing the police of racism, and being profoundly uncooperative. Hence the arrest.

The Cambridge police couldn't have stumbled upon a more unfortunate individual with whom to have a run-in. Gates is a friend of President Obama. He is also the director of Harvard's W.E.B. Du Bois Institute for African and African-American Research—which translates into his being one of the "Marxist professors" with whom Obama admits he went out of his way to align himself while in college, according to his book *Dreams from My Father.*

You'll have to forgive me (well, actually, you don't) if I'm not impressed by the fact that Gates is considered one of America's pre-eminent black scholars, and that he was once noted as one of *Time* magazine's most influential people. As such, I don't see him as being any more than an agent of the negrophiliac social convention that keeps black Americans resentful, desperate, ignorant, impoverished, and—oh, yes—voting for progressives.

It's also the same convention that got Obama elected, while we're at it.

When police officials discovered who Gates was (regarding his position and credentials), they recommended the charges be dropped against him. In my view, this was a mistake; he had been duly charged, and reversing themselves only made the Cambridge police appear blameworthy.

But it was already too late. Not only was Gates gibbering to anyone who would listen respecting the "racist treatment" he had received from police, but his buddy, President Obama, had weighed in with his own Anglophobic, anti-law-enforcement drivel, declaring that the police had acted "stupidly."

When I was a teen, my father admonished me sharply respecting any interactions I might have with police, particularly when I started driving. It was the early 1970s, I had long hair, and we lived in New York, where police could get strung pretty tight due to the sort of customers they encountered on a regular basis. My dad knew that it was a possibility I might run into a belligerent or even a racist cop.

His warning was as follows: "No matter what, always speak calmly and respectfully. You can't sue if you're dead."

I thank God and my dad for that advice. I wound up defusing more situations with police using that method than I can now reliably recount, some with officers who were champing at the bit for a confrontation.

Conversely, I have never—*ever*—seen a black man who was stopped by police fail to get mouthy. By all accounts, prior to Gates's arrest, he had devolved from a respected professor with vast accomplishments and education, into a gangbanger from the television show *Cops*.

Why? Because paranoid Anglophobia, anti-law-enforcementism, and anti-Americanism is this guy's stock-in-trade. Gates has spent his entire career infusing college students with the dogma of America being a racist nation with racist police who are ever itching to abuse blacks.

Contrary to the belief of America's deluded masses—that of President Obama having been raised on the Kansas farm next to Dorothy's—he was also raised on paranoid Anglophobia, anti-law-enforcementism, and anti-Americanism. His slip was a significant indicator of who the man really is; he is one of many black Americans (as well as progressives in general) who have been conditioned to believe that all police are closet storm troopers.

By the end of that week, Obama's statement had become the media story due to the outcry from outraged police agencies the nation over, so much so that he was compelled to hold a press conference to address the issue. As he explained his stupid "stupidly" remark away, Obama reminded us that black Americans are "sensitive" apropos the police and racism. On that point, he was correct; today, it is largely because of people like him and all of the other race-baiting, influential blacks for whom perpetuating the myth of America being a racist nation has been an imperative for decades.

THE "JENA SIX"

Jena, Louisiana (CNN, September 19, 2007): *There is no link between the nooses hung by white students outside a Louisiana high school and the alleged beating of a white student by black teens, according to the U.S. attorney who reviewed investigations into the incidents.*

Some residents say nooses hung from a tree on campus sparked the violence that landed the Jena 6 in jail.

"The Jena Six": It even sounds like the sixties, which is exactly where the media and the poverty pimps (the aforementioned professional civil-rights activists) want to keep America in spirit.

"Enough is Enough!" said the T-shirts.

"Free the Jena 6!" the crowds chanted.

Here is an example of negrophilia manifesting a double standard regarding law enforcement and the legal system: On August 31, 2006, a black student at Jena High School sat in the shade of a tree frequented by white students at the school. Later, three nooses were found hanging from the tree.

Scott Windham, the school's principal, recommended expulsion of three white teens identified as the responsible parties, but was overruled by the school superintendent and board members, who (yes, idiotically) put the matter down as a "prank." The three students were given three-day suspensions.

Unsurprisingly, racial tensions flared at the school and in Jena that fall. On November 30, 2006, part of the school was destroyed by a suspected arson fire. Other minor altercations and fistfights were reported; one black student was attacked at a party by white students.

On December 4, 2006, a fight broke out in the high school lunchroom between a white student, Justin Barker, and a black student. Barker was rendered unconscious, then kicked and stomped by a group of black students as he lay motionless. Five of the teens were later charged as adults with attempted second-degree murder. A sixth teen was charged as a juvenile.

Mychal Bell, one of the five, was convicted in June 2007 on a reduced charge. Shortly before his sentencing, an appeals court vacated the conviction on the grounds that the charges should have been brought in juvenile court.

As the result of a massive e-mail campaign begun by the NAACP, which tied in Bell's conviction to the noose incident, the series of events began to gain national attention. Alarmist, inflammatory media circulated by the NAACP describing Jena as a "highly segregated rural Louisiana town" fanned the flames, which were subsequently drenched with accelerant by the press.

"This is not about race," Rev. Al Sharpton said when he arrived on the scene in Jena. "This is not about politics. This is not a march against whites or against Jena. It's not about black and white."

Right . . . it was about Al Sharpton getting more face time.

The facts don't matter when one is dealing with another Al "waste of nucleic acids" Sharpton production, which the march on September 20, 2006, in Jena essentially became. Equating this unfortunate phenomenon with legitimate civil-rights events of old, and misleading blacks vis-à-vis its origins and significance was insulting and obscene.

Public officials in Jena were about as contrite as they could have been regarding the noose incident, and clear about their wish that the school superintendent and board should have elected to punish those responsible more harshly. Fortunately, they did maintain their claim that the severity of the reaction to the trial of the "Jena Six" was activist- and media-driven.

The press did not reveal that Mychal Bell, who was convicted of battery in the Barker beating, had been convicted a year earlier for battery and committed *three* additional crimes while on probation, making the Jena Six verdict his *fifth* conviction for a crime of violence.

Like I say, so much for the facts . . .

Incidentally, my car was tagged with racial epithets some years ago in the predominantly white city where I live. I might have made all sorts of presumptions about the incident, called out the police and the press, and stared down every one of my white neighbors for months on end. It turned out that the tagging was done by a young black moron who lived a few doors down and thought I acted "too white." The point is that white bigots have no monopoly whatsoever on this sort of thing.

The Jena Six example illustrates one of innumerable examples of the pendulum having swung too far in the desired direction. If one scrutinizes the summative aspects of this case, the noose episode becomes almost incidental. The perpetrators in the beating were essentially looking for an excuse to do violence, and it is impossible to tell if, or to what degree, the previous developments at Jena High had influenced the beating. Given the noose factor—and, we cannot forget, the media hype surrounding it—the incident became about alleged ethnic harassment. Once again, opportunistic activists asserted that white racism was to blame, and so, lawfully prosecuting a sociopathic thug became nearly impossible, *because of his race.*

Does this sound like a society in which the law enforcement and judicial decks are stacked against blacks?

THE DUKE LACROSSE CASE

On March 13, 2006, Crystal Gail Mangum, a black stripper and "escort" who was also a student at North Carolina Central University, entertained members of the Duke Blue Devils men's lacrosse team at an off-campus party. Within days, Mangum charged that three members of the team had orchestrated her gang-rape.

The case resulted in a massive and immediate media feeding frenzy, and public outcry nationwide. With no evidence other than Ms. Mangum's word, millions of Americans accepted the gruesome picture that was subsequently painted depicting her being brutalized and sexually assaulted by a drunken, hooting gang of testosterone-saturated young brutes—all of them white.

Among those who presumed the athletes' guilt was the district attorney for Durham County, North Carolina, Mike Nifong. Yes, he agreed with all of outraged black America: It had been a *hate crime,* most foul.

Leaving aside the question of guilt or innocence in the case—which had by no means been established—there was never any debate over whether the rape of a black woman by white men should indeed be considered a hate crime. After all, black men are not typically charged with hate crimes when they rape white women. Rape is rape, right?

Apparently not. Given the gusto with which Nifong prepared to prosecute the case, the press, many Americans, and even factions within the Duke University community already had the young men convicted. Duke's president canceled the remainder of the 2006 lacrosse season, and the principal suspects and their families became something beneath personae non gratae.

The rape case itself didn't develop so well, though. The timeline of Mangum's stated activities that night didn't hold up to scrutiny. Her statements kept changing. Photos taken at the party showed Mangum and a coworker having a great old time with the lacrosse team. It was verified via cell phone records and a store's video surveillance camera that one of the suspects wasn't even at the house during the alleged assault. The rape kit didn't turn up any DNA evidence from the suspects, but it did turn up semen from at least two other men. At a time designated as after the alleged assault but before Mangum went to police, she was observed by police passed out drunk in a car. It also turned out that the twenty-seven-year-old Mangum had a criminal record that included grand theft auto.

All the while, the suspects and their families asserted that the athletes were innocent of the charges. For the most part, no one listened.

Then, some pundits and members of the press began to wonder whether Nifong was pursuing the Duke case in order to win a re-election in Durham, which had a substantial black community presence. Their wondering became questions verbalized, and then Nifong's actions began to be scrutinized. The holes in Mangum's story became public, and finally horrendous misconduct on the district attorney's part came to light. He was essentially preparing to railroad the three suspects in order to secure the future of his office.

In April of 2007, all charges against members of the lacrosse team were dropped. Mike Nifong withdrew from the case as the North Carolina State Bar filed ethics charges against him. Shortly thereafter, he was disbarred, and later convicted of criminal contempt in the case.

Certainly, the lion's share of the blame here can be placed on one man's ambition. It wouldn't be the first time a DA or other public figure had used the criminal justice system to further their own political ends. However, Nifong would not have had the resources and justification to pursue the case had it not been for negrophilia. The press and activists would not have been able to stoke the fires of resentment and race hatred had it not been for these pervasive sensibilities.

The entirety of this tragedy, save for Mangum's initial allegations, could not have occurred were it not for the effects of negrophilia on our society and upon those involved.

AL SHARPTON AND TAWANA BRAWLEY

Few people from outside the New York metropolitan area are aware that the incidents which follow are essentially Rev. Al Sharpton's claim to fame, but there it is. It is a chief reason that his detractors (such as myself) believe that he possesses no credibility whatsoever, nor should he be validated, certified, or otherwise endorsed by anyone who wishes to maintain any measure of credibility themselves.

On November 28, 1987, Tawana Brawley, a fifteen-year-old who had been missing for four days, was found in a state of insensibility, partly inside a garbage bag near a former residence in Wappingers Falls, New York. Her clothing was in tatters, her body had been smeared with feces, and racial epithets had been scrawled on her upper body.

Upon questioning, Brawley claimed that she had been raped and left in that condition by six white men, some of whom were local police officers. One was a New York prosecutor. The Reverend Al, who had just begun to get media attention, swept in with activist attorneys Alton H. Maddox and C. Vernon Mason to "support" Brawley. The liberal New York press, which has served to poison race relations to no mean degree for decades, relayed a play-by-play account of the legal wrangling, with Sharpton as the point man.

There was one problem: Brawley had made up the story to deflect attention from her own recent irresponsible and delinquent behavior. The grand jury seated to hear the case apparently saw through the thin veneer of her account, and one year later ruled that Brawley had not been the victim of a sexual assault; further, they were of the opinion she'd concocted the whole thing, staging everything from the venue to the "body art" and feces-smearing.

That's not the worst part: Since the case had gotten so much attention, and Sharpton had been so deeply involved, it became painfully evident to the public—and obviously the court—that he had known Brawley's yarn was a sham. Sharpton, Maddox, and Mason were sued for slander and defamation of character by Steven Pagones, the prosecutor whom Brawley had named as one of her alleged assailants. Sharpton and his cohorts were ordered to pay $345,000 in damages. To this day, there are activists and politicians in New York who tout Brawley's account as factual, and the slander convictions as a gross miscarriage of justice.

These examples are but a few of the more prominent illustrations of the subversion of the criminal justice system that has transpired in the years since the civil rights movement. Yes, we do have an inordinately high percentage of blacks in our prisons, but this is due to blacks having been targeted by activists and lawmakers in the manner described in this chapter. Had these foes simply gotten "out of the way," as Ronald Reagan might have put it, blacks' advancement over these decades would have more resembled the slingshot effect. The degree to which fear of blacks versus the need for their political support, factored into the policies formulated and programs enacted, is all but immaterial at this point; the result—which has only benefited activists and politicians—remains the same.

The progressives, guilty-feeling whites, and angry blacks that comprise the general population are among the same who wind up within the criminal justice system as judges, attorneys, prosecutors, defendants, police, and victims. Police wind up intimidated, fearful of charges of brutality, unappreciated, and maligned. It is quite likely that the effects of the Racism Is Good scenario detailed in Chapter Six contribute to the making of racist police officers. Prosecutors find themselves hamstrung due to negrophilia and political correctness, or overwhelmed beyond their ability to cope.

The overall structure has indeed been turned on its head. In the military, they have a term that denotes something that has been knocked out of kilter beyond all recognition. It employs profane vernacular, the first part of which is "cluster." This is our legal system as it relates to black Americans, and it has grown out of negrophilia. Blacks are simply suffering in a different manner than prior to the Civil Rights Movement, but the effect is somehow supposed to be overlooked due to all of the ostensibly good intentions.

Often, the guilty go free, or are not prosecuted at all. The system as an organism actually breeds racism, particularly when one reaches the level of penitentiaries. As one might imagine, within this paradigm, justice for the victims of crimes, regardless of race, is often the last issue considered. The entire system (which of course is controlled from afar by soulless, faceless whites) is under perpetual indictment— and often from the same parties—for both neglecting crime in black neighborhoods, then "persecuting" perpetrators when they finally make it into courtrooms.

With my own ears I have heard defense attorneys make specious, non sequitur arguments for their clients based on the past oppression of blacks, or the drug addiction of a parent in the face of crimes for which a white person would be cast into the penitentiary without a second look. And like other offenders who are sentenced to light terms, or none at all, by lenient judges, and who offend again, the number of blacks who have been allowed to rack up new victims is incalculable—but in this instance, the leniency comes about because they are black.

Efforts toward changing this state of affairs have been resisted, and will continue to be for the foreseeable future, because to do so would be to the detriment of the system at large, and to the power players within it.

ELEVEN

negrophilia in foreign policy

NEGROPHILIA IN AMERICAN foreign policy has had a farther-reaching effect than the domestic variety, implausible though this may seem. Why? Simply because the effect of negrophilia on the American people has translated into modifications in U.S. foreign policy, charitable giving and lobbying, and this affects millions outside the United States. Inasmuch as the same Americans who interact with each other on a daily basis also govern the criminal justice system, so do they manage those agencies that administer foreign policy. In short, the same executives, lawmakers, and appointees in Washington who have made a shambles of our domestic situation have also done so with American foreign policy. Changes in their attitudes regarding blacks and other minorities—as well as the fallacy and mythology—have been conveyed onto other nations in which nonwhites predominate.

Once again, the effect of negrophilia in foreign policy is another subject upon which volumes could be written. Here, I only seek to convey the hows, whys, and poignant manifestations.

Negrophilia in foreign policy extends beyond concepts of mere relations with black people; it is an extension of the concept that people of color and those in undeveloped nations abroad have been exploited by whites, for which we (Americans) are obliged to collectively make restitution. The erroneous beliefs detailed in these chapters have had incalculable consequences respecting the way in which Americans view people of color abroad, and the way our nation officially deals with them. Some of these manifestations are obvious, others are far more insidious.

It has become painfully evident in the last few years more than at any other point in American history our electorate, and even more so the general public, are woefully uninformed relative to civic and political issues. This has been exacerbated by more than a generation of Marxist-influenced, government-run education, and corrupted institutions of higher learning, some of which, by design, have been advancing a substandard and sociopolitically biased worldview. Hence, some of the fallacious and dangerous beliefs pertaining to race politics in the domestic area have been superimposed onto Americans' overview of geopolitics.

First, a disclaimer: Inasmuch as domestic policy in the U.S. once possessed certain retrograde, ill-formed, and unjust concepts and practices, so then did our foreign policy. America's foreign policy has been marred with every bit as many stupid and imprudent actions and programs as its homeland policies. The purpose here is not to enumerate them or to engage in acts of contrition for our mistakes. Suffice it to say that many were made; this chapter is concerned with the fact that our foreign policy in the area of race consciousness, like our domestic policy, has swung too far in the opposite direction when our statesmen and women and our lawmakers sought to clean the slate. Much of this has been part and parcel of the principles that have been incrementally insinuated into our foreign policy by the left, which has sought to compromise America's preeminence on the world stage.

I turn once again to the treasonous conduct of the Congressional Black Caucus as an extreme example of blacks indoctrinated into far-left dogma influencing U.S. foreign policy. Not only does this body have leave to take unscheduled holidays to Cuba, validating the regime and implying ubiquitous public support, but such bodies are able to directly affect foreign policy. They are congressmen, after all. At the time of this writing, two prominent members of the U.S. House Committee on Foreign Affairs are the far-left Diane Watson (D-CA) and Keith Ellison, the Muslim from Minnesota.

As Sherif Ali ibn el Kharish informed T.E. Lawrence in the 1962 film *Lawrence of Arabia*: There are no Arabs, and there never have been. From the outside looking in, there *appears* to be a race commonly referred to as "Arabs"; these are in truth multitudinous tribes and clans who have been struggling for preeminence in the region for many millennia.

This was most recently illustrated during and after the downfall of Saddam Hussein, whose minority Tikriti clan ruled Iraq with the proverbial iron fist. The same tribal dynamic remains in play throughout the Middle East, Africa, and much of Asia.

The decline of imperialism as Western historians understand it (as opposed to international socialists) began with the Hussein-McMahon Correspondence of 1916, the agreement between Britain (via Sir Henry McMahon, British high commissioner in Egypt at the time) and the sharif of Mecca (Hussein ibn Ali) that if "Arabs" successfully revolted against the Ottoman Empire, Britain would support claims for their independence—whatever that meant.

In this, which became known as Pan-Arabism, Britannia began that transformation from an imperialist nation to a scraping one. The British Empire had a longer history of imperialism than the United States, whose leaders saw that imperialist practices were becoming out of vogue at the same time it was becoming a world power. Thus, although powerful Western nations maintained strong foreign policy for a time, intellectual dishonesty with respect to objectives and world opinion led to weak commitment in these areas. These, I believe, were among the seeds of such things as negrophilia and political correctness. Nations and races wouldn't be enslaved or exploited outright, but they would remain second-class. The advent of socialism and Marxist thought lent more fuel to the fires of resentment and suspicion between developed and underdeveloped nations.

The recent threats against the West by al-Qaida, along with Iran's defiance relative to its nuclear buildup, make a strong case for the imperialism practiced by nations like Britain, France, and Holland in times of old.

We cannot turn the clock back, but it occurs to me that such policies might have prevented the necessity for the War on Terror. This would have required the will of Western nations, but these unfortunately had begun to operate under the naïve notion that third world nations would muster the wisdom and willingness to adopt democratic concepts of liberty, justice, and benevolence simply because the West desired it.

Suppose that the West had correctly realized that, despite our healthy respect for others' right to self-determination, our lofty ideals were not likely to be easily or quickly embraced by cultures in which these principles had not naturally evolved. Suppose further that instead of outright exploitation of these nations and the support of dictators who would dance to our tune in the short run (which, of course, led to resentment and revolt under our weakening socialist-influenced foreign policy), we had realized that our high regard for the self-determination of others made imperialism a moral imperative—if, perhaps, imperialism of a different kind.

Might it have been more prudent—and intellectually honest—to have maintained true puppet governments in the third world, but with the social, economic—and, yes, military—provisions in place necessary to acclimatize these cultures to Western concepts, rather than simply exploiting them economically and then withdrawing when the chips were down?

Am I saying that a program of culturally colonizing the third world in a systematic and deliberate fashion would have been an appropriate course of action? Should we have kept underdeveloped nations "down" rather than allowing them the self-determination we so highly value?

Though it may be something of a digression: Yes—that is exactly what I am saying. Societies that eschew slavery, mass execution, stoning, rape as a criminal penalty, beheading, and impalement are—to be blunt—culturally superior to those that do not. It was the West's moral obligation to see that overwhelming economic and military power did not fall into the hands of culturally immature societies, but lack of conviction, moral weakness, and intellectual dishonesty caused us to drop the ball.

For the record, despite all that has been done in the areas of humanitarian, economic, and military aid, the nations in question *still* accuse the West of having "kept them down." It's one of the reasons so many of them want to kill us at present.

It is this sort of misplaced respect for self-determination—which blacks in America were just beginning to be allowed—that began to compromise U.S. foreign policy. Rather than operating out of our national interest—which most nations do—the immature and irrational worldview of activists, progressives in Washington, and a public that was frankly, rather spoiled, won the day.

∽

A convicting and sad instance of the failure of American foreign policy, and how flawed concepts of race relations have affected same, lies in the example of the island nation of Haiti.

The Republic of Haiti is situated on the western side of the island of Hispaniola in the Caribbean, the eastern side being occupied by the Dominican Republic. Though discovered by Christopher Columbus in 1492, it was settled by Frenchmen, primarily in the 1600s. As with many of the islands in the Caribbean, its original inhabitants were Arawak Indians, who were more or less bred out by the whites and black slaves who began arriving on the island in 1517. Haiti holds the distinction of having been the only nation in the region that was liberated as a result of a slave rebellion; this was led by François-Dominique Toussaint L'Ouverture in 1797.

Although opinions as to why the following occurred are diverse, in 1915 the United States occupied Haiti. One rationale (some claim pretext) for this action was the inordinate economic influence German nationals living in Haiti had acquired. In actuality, there were other reasons, both economic and strategic (some would claim "imperialist").

In any case, for the next nineteen years, the U.S. occupied that nation. Haiti owed the U.S. a bunch of money at the time, and efforts were made to stabilize the country economically as well as politically.

One of the many things the American government did not understand is one that has already been pointed out here: Haiti is a racially caste-based society, caught between Napoleonism and Africanism. Over the next two decades, the U.S. carelessly poured economic and military aid into Haiti, essentially educating the military and ruling class in the efficient ways of the West—just enough training to make them dangerous. It was through this edification that the various monumentally corrupt dictators and provisional governments that came about (as noted earlier, composed mainly of the mulatto class) were able to oppress the black majority with twentieth-century efficiency. In 1957, François Duvalier came to power. In 1964, he declared himself president for life. A twentieth-century despot of legendary proportions, "Papa Doc" Duvalier founded the infamous Milice de Volontaires de la Sécurité Nationale (MVSN), or Tonton Macoutes, a private paramilitary police organization patterned after elite units to which the Haitian military had been exposed while being trained by the U.S. Marines. The Tonton Macoutes were, of course, legendary for their brutality, and serve as one of our archetypes for corruption and viciousness in third world dictatorships.

The Haiti fiasco is one of the greatest bungles of American foreign policy, perhaps all the more shameful because it occurred so close to home. While a degree of the mismanagement was a result of paternalism and a noncommittal brand of imperialism, much was due to misjudgment of the Haitian people on the part of the American government. In the beginning of the endeavor, the U.S. was an emerging world power, and undeniably operating in a more imperialist modality. Of course the Haitians were black, and in 1915, they did not receive much more respect or deference than American blacks. In short, some of the U.S. policies were racist. Toward the end of America's direct involvement, however, popular attitudes in the U.S. were beginning to change, and imperialism was waning. As with other emerging and undeveloped nations with which the U.S. has been involved, in the end we withdrew and left the Haitians to their own questionable devices. Our interference only served to exacerbate their problems, and the results affect Haiti to this day. Though the U.S. and other nations have been pouring aid and investment capital into Haiti over the last few decades, Port-au-Poverty (that would be its capital, Port-au-*Prince*) remains one of the most impoverished cities in the Western Hemisphere. As is widely reported, bands of Haitians on dangerously unstable rafts routinely (and often unsuccessfully) brave the eight-hundred-mile ocean voyage to Florida in hope of a life in the U.S., even as an illegal immigrant.

Almost one hundred years later, the U.S. government still chronically makes the mistake of superimposing its perception of American blacks—though by now it has changed drastically—onto the Haitian people; "'our blacks' behave in such a way, so let's have a go with those Haitians again." In 1986, protests against Jean-Claude "Baby Doc" Duvalier (Papa Doc's son) forced the Duvalier family into exile. A new constitution was drafted and approved, and for the next four years, the nation attempted to have elections that were usually aborted due to violence. In 1990, Jean-Bertrand Aristide, a former priest, won the election by an overwhelming majority. He was a popular figure, gaining good press in the West and actually engendering hope in many who had given up on the island nation.

Unfortunately, Aristide, despite his status as a cleric, had little more idea of what a democratic Haiti would look like—assuming he cared—than a housecat. Less than a year later, Aristide faced a no-confidence vote and was forced into exile. During President Bill Clinton's administration, U.S. troops landed in Haiti, supposedly to "stabilize" the country once again. Aristide was restored to power, despite the fact that it was now well-known that he was a thug, as well as being anti-capitalist and anti-American; apparently his stance as a member of the radical left outweighed these factors.

Corruption and thuggery are simply the Haitian way, and Haitians are quite used to it. At this juncture, there is also the pervasive influence of the "Catholic left" at work; as with some Catholic activists in the West, social justice proponents and liberation theology mavens who glean power—and, of course, as much foreign aid from the U.S. and European Union as they can—via preaching the same message of Western oppression and past injustices that black activists spread in America.

In Haiti, regarding American intervention, the issue has been our wholly failing to consider that which Western governments fail to consider again and again: Democracy can seldom be simply transplanted; it must develop. This is not to say that an individual from a third world nation, or one with a different form of government, cannot appreciate democracy and assimilate in the West, but reasoning that a culture operating in the third or seventeenth century will enthusiastically embrace democracy simply because it is an equitable, logical choice is not a realistic expectation.

This assessment of the United States' involvement in Haiti may sound like anti-American propaganda, but I believe that while it is important to be honest about America's cultural superiority in certain areas, it is equally important to be honest pertaining to the mistakes that have been made, and for which the American people are often called upon to collectively pay.

While the case of Haiti may not be a specific example of negrophilia per se, it is an ancillary illustration of the sort of "groupthink" that leads to harmful policies, both foreign and domestic.

One of the more topical manifestations of negrophilia in the degradation of Western foreign policy was illustrated by the reign of the flamboyant (and probably quite insane) African dictator Idi Amin, who ruled Uganda from 1971 to 1979. Due to the advent of Western policies previously described, the British lost control of their proxy government there in 1966. A former swimmer, boxing champion, and cook in the British colonial army, Amin first came on the radar of the establishment media during his military coup (in 1971). Soon after, he grabbed headlines by placing a British journalist under house arrest for criticizing his regime. The British government was forced to issue an apology in order for the man to regain his freedom.

While this led to a customary portrayal of Amin as a comic and occasionally endearing figure in the press, there was nothing funny about him. During his reign, it is estimated that he killed between fifty thousand and half a million people, many of them from rival ethnic groups, including political opponents, journalists, religious leaders, students, and foreign nationals. On one occasion, bodies clogged the Nile River so severely that water treatment and sewage facilities were impacted. In 1972, Amin ordered all Asians living in Uganda— around eighty thousand of them—deported. He seized their businesses, which represented a significant percentage of the Ugandan economy. As a result, the economy collapsed.

A supporter of Islamic terror in the region, Amin once declared that Hitler had been correct in attempting to exterminate every Jew in Europe. Despite countless eyewitness accounts of Amin's atrocities, they are routinely denied, disputed, and otherwise downplayed by the Western press.

Dubbed "The Butcher of Uganda," his savagery became legendary; only the most heinous and appalling documentable instances of his behavior are mentioned here. It was only a matter of time before the tribalist Amin became adventurous (as would his colleague Saddam Hussein a few years later). In 1977, after Tanzania granted asylum to some key Ugandan dissidents, Amin summarily annexed a portion of that nation. Between the retaliation and growing dissidence within Uganda, the situation deteriorated to the point where Amin was forced to flee in 1979. He died in exile in 2003.

The point here—other than it seems Uganda might have been better off under British rule—is that the perception of those in the West was (and remains) colored by their superficiality and modern perceptions of fairness and parity. The fact is that Amin wasn't "The Hitler of Africa," as some would later portray him; he really was a pretty garden variety African despot. There were probably thousands of Ugandans at that time who would have behaved similarly had they come to power.

∽

In the mid-1970s, Western support for the African Republic of Rhodesia crumbled. The West, and Britain in particular, which had ruled the area as a colony from the 1880s until 1965, objected to the government's policies and its insistence on maintaining control from within the white minority. After a civil war against the government, led by Marxists Joshua Nkomo and Robert Mugabe, Rhodesia became Zimbabwe in 1979. The nation, led by Mugabe, has been in decline ever since. Mugabe redistributed land to people who could not farm it, which led to a decline in agricultural exports, and a stultified economy. Drought, disease, and starvation in poor sectors still plague what was once a modern, Westernized country.

The transformation of South Africa during the period from 1990 through 1994 came about similarly. Despite the endemic barbarity practiced in African nations, during the 1980s, the average news watcher might have developed the idea that the South African system of apartheid was the most odious atrocity devised by humankind. Granted, it was immoral, but the decline in the economy since democratic elections were first held in 1994 has only been ameliorated by the vastness of that nation's resources.

All of these developments have come about due to aspects of negrophilia and ancillary progressive ideals. Social changes that took place on the domestic front gave rise to the uniquely twentieth-century Western notion that "blacks should have Africa," regardless of whether they run it into the ground, support terrorism, or destabilize economies, or if their leaders are exponentially more monstrous than their European predecessors.

∽

Listen and understand! That terminator is out there.
It can't be bargained with. It can't be reasoned with.
It doesn't feel pity, or remorse, or fear and it absolutely will not stop,
ever, until you are dead!
—Kyle Reese, from the film *The Terminator*

Sound like anyone you've heard of? Perhaps a network of killers we've been "unofficially" at war with since September 11, 2001—though in actuality, far longer than that? Not quite as formidable as Terminators, to be sure; still, our moral and political weakness has empowered Islamic fascists far more than any resolve or resources they possess.

There is irony in my use of a quote from a major Hollywood film. Though the entertainment industry has indeed provided Americans with poignant, memorable messages and memories over the years, its influence on our culture has devolved into something manifestly destructive and, in its present form, must not be allowed to continue. Hollywood has become essentially an extension of the news media (employers of those in Hollywood and the mainstream press often being one and the same), itself a propaganda arm of the left. If U.S. laws regarding sedition were being applied as intended when they were written, there would be at least a few dozen prominent American entertainers in prison with possibly hundreds of news bureau chiefs.

In a column I penned a few years back (during G. W. Bush's second term) addressing the War on Terror and Israel's incursion into Lebanon after attacks by Hezbollah, reader responses I received from those who disagreed with me made me wonder if they'd even read the article. To simplify, their reasoning consisted of "Yes, buts." "Yes, but Bush this. Yes, but our foreign policy that." It was as though I was listening to the half-baked, outcome-focused logic of a back-talking seven-year-old . . .

To the Islamic fascist, Westerners (and Americans in particular) have been utterly dehumanized; we are vermin, something to be destroyed with the righteous determination with which one annihilates an infestation of roaches. Feeble (and often grossly fallacious) theoretical arguments and vapid intellectualism has led me to wonder if Americans believe that they would somehow be spared if Islamic fascists had the facility to rain paratroopers upon our cities and towns. I muse over how they would reason their way out of seeing their families raped, one by one, then having a turn at being raped before their heads were sawed off.

Americans are entitled to their own opinions, and to express them. There's also nothing unlawful about being a fool. But the intellectual delusion that exists in America regarding the reality of where we actually stand, and what we stand for, has become dangerously rampant.

The snide, acerbic armchair generals with journalism degrees, and no conception whatsoever of the mind of the enemy or effective measures of dealing with him, have long since crossed the line between free speech and treason—as have too many of our entertainers.

From whence did these imprudent, reckless beliefs come? It's quite likely that you've figured it out by now. As with the humanitarian consciousness Americans developed on the domestic front, encouraged by madmen in the press, we shot past the middle ground again. We went from abject ignorance of what was being done in the name of American interests to cultivating an inordinate sympathy for all little brown peoples of the world, even if they possessed a retrograde culture or wished us ill. This was exacerbated by the insinuation of Marxist thought into our worldview, wherein anyone with a profit motive is a devil.

In July of 2008, *WorldNetDaily*'s Bob Unruh reported on S. 2433, the "Global Poverty Act of 2007." This $845 billion planet-wide welfare program, introduced by then-Senator Barack Obama, would "require the president to develop and implement a comprehensive strategy to further the United States foreign policy objective of promoting the reduction of global poverty, the elimination of extreme global poverty, and the achievement of the Millennium Development Goal of reducing by one-half the proportion of people worldwide, between 1990 and 2015, who live on less than $1 per day."

While it was less expensive than the American Recovery and Reinvestment Act of 2009 or the various health care "reform" proposals submitted by Congress and the Obama administration during that year, this is what comes from fifty years of a Marxist-inspired educational system and the insidious machinations of a far-left press— a situation wherein most average Americans are wholly ignorant of basic economic principles, and wherein their attention is being deftly misdirected from historical facts.

The chief fallacy that has been promoted by the left since the early twentieth century is, in lay terms, as follows: There is but one "pie," as it were, of capital and resources of all types; at any given time it tends to be inequitably divided, and citizens need government to ensure that it is more equitably divided. This, of course, is pure Marxism.

The free market model—the accurate one—is that there are many "pies," and more are being created on a continual basis, providing that individuals and businesses are allowed the freedom to do so. Microsoft Corporation, Ben and Jerry's, and microbreweries are but a few examples of enterprises that demonstrated this paving of vast new inroads within existing industries.

Whether addressing domestic or global fronts, the proof that throwing money at the problem of poverty never works is beyond overwhelming; it is as clear as the concept that shooting heroin into one's arm is probably not a constructive idea. Yet, at a juncture where many Americans are truly suffering economically, a president is not only able to get away with proposing multi-billion- and trillion-dollar bequests and programs, he is lauded for it.

The people of the United States of America are the world's greatest charitable givers. As it stands, our government weighs in ahead of the governments of other developed nations in this area. Still, those who make such generosity possible—working Americans—find themselves with nowhere to turn when they run into difficulty themselves. I would rather see the mortgages of every American family currently under threat of foreclosure brought current before one more illegal immigrant is given free medical care, one more fiscally irresponsible corporation is bailed out, or one more dollar falls into the hands of a third world despot.

I remind the reader of "Oil for Food": Billions of American dollars were appropriated for the program that allowed Saddam Hussein's Iraq to sell oil on the world market in order to obtain humanitarian aid, ostensibly to ameliorate the suffering of Iraqi citizens due to international economic sanctions against Iraq. It became a global scandal, with white-collar criminals, gangsters, international arms dealers, and the Hussein regime enriching themselves on the aforementioned financial resources. S. 2433 was a similar proposed massive money grab being sold on the basis of false compassion and unwarranted guilt—nothing more. There have been many less pricey foreign aid cons perpetrated over the years by politicians on both sides of the aisle. The Global Poverty Act would have represented further confiscatory taxation of the American people in order to provide billions in circumlocutory appeasement for third world governments, with the obligatory administrative "lost billions" appropriated by corrupt dictators, lawmakers, consultants, and United Nations bandits—and Barack Obama knew it. Fortunately, it did not become law for a variety of reasons, among them being the possibility that the entire proposal was actually intended to ingratiate Obama to his political base prior to the 2008 election.

The central question is this: Why does Obama, or any of the hundreds of lawmakers or members of the executive branch who have proposed similar measures over the last forty years, even have the gall to suggest such abortions?

The answer is in variants of this book's thesis, which hold that *we owe it to them.*

∽

Socialism or death! We shall prevail!
—Venezuelan dictator Hugo Chavez, January 2007,
at the inauguration for his third term

I didn't feel particularly confident with our government's policies concerning our enemies prior to the Democratic takeover of Congress in 2006; now, I'm even less inclined to feel so.

In a column published in October of 2006, I flat out stated that evangelist and former presidential candidate Pat Robertson had been right when he called for the assassination of Hugo Chavez, despite the fact that Robertson later apologized when the Thought Police descended upon him. Chavez, a megalomaniac who quotes Castro, claims that Christ was a socialist, wants to head up his own "church," courts Iranian president Mahmoud Ahmadinejad, and refers to his own country as "The Fatherland," is apparently just another guy—even an admirable, forward-thinking leader in the eyes of the establishment press, a substantial number of American lawmakers, and even President Obama.

In the main, conscientious Americans respect the rule of law almost to a fault. The only law despots, megalomaniacs, and retrograde fanatics understand, however, is the law of the jungle. They do not respect life or liberty as the average American does—and we'd damned well better get that through our heads, and fast. In addition to the day-to-day abject misery they inflict on their own people (usually while deflecting blame toward the U.S.), they are capable of committing atrocities that most Americans can barely conceptualize.

There is not now, nor has there ever been, any exception to the law of the jungle, nor any successful circumventing thereof—regardless of how much sympathy Americans have for the little brown people of the world.

TWELVE

negrophilia and political correctness

Politically correct: conforming to a belief that language and practices which could offend political sensibilities (as in matters of sex or race) should be eliminated.
—MERRIAM-WEBSTER DICTIONARY

T HE READER MAY find it horrifying to learn that the term "politically correct" (PC) even has an entry in dictionaries. Be that as it may, while the institution of negrophilia was in place long before the phrase "political correctness" came into common use, nascent stages of the latter paved the way for the former. Meaning that, negrophilia could not have developed had certain concepts that would later coalesce into PC not already been sold to the public. As presented earlier, some of the positive stereotypes that now exist regarding blacks are every bit as ludicrous as negative ones to which some people used to hold, and it is the same pliancy, born of guilt, that allows such beliefs to develop.

It is difficult, for example, to think of Adolf Hitler as someone who had "the best of intentions" that somehow went woefully awry. It is doubtful that many sound-minded people would argue that Josef Stalin had good intentions; he and Hitler were thugs who conned the masses. But many of the people who put them in power started out with good intentions. The question is: If the actions in question result in untold suffering, does it matter to the sufferers whether or not those who took said action had good intentions?

The model of so-called "political correctness," such as it is under-stood in America, was practically made to reinforce concepts such as negrophilia. In fact, it is a more widespread use of many of the same warped principles applied to a larger scope of factions and ideas with favored status. First off, it probably has not escaped notice of the more well-read that PC possesses an uncanny similarity to the concept of "doublethink" from George Orwell's novel *1984*. Part of what is frightening about PC is that we *did* have the evil model of double-think to reference from that book.

Yet political correctness has taken hold nevertheless . . .

Don't you see that the whole aim of Newspeak is to narrow the range of thought? Has it ever occurred to you, Winston, that by the year 2050, at the very latest, not a single human being will be alive who could understand such a conversation as we are having now? The whole climate of thought will be different. In fact, there will be no thought, as we understand it now. Orthodoxy means not thinking— not needing to think. Orthodoxy is unconsciousness.
—From *1984*, by GEORGE ORWELL

The year 1984 came and went, but the vision of Orwell's *1984* is more germane with respect to the current state of American society than ever. I recall that marketers sort of worked up to 1984 (the year) with a resurgence of interest in *1984* (the book). The film was remade starring John Hurt, and sales of Orwell's novel climbed. I first read the book during the mid-70s, and it chilled me.

1984 was—and still is, in my estimation—the first great dystopian classic: a story of a cold, evil regime in which the individual lived only to serve the state and its aims, and in which the individual was subli-mated entirely. Since then, a generation has come of age that may not have even heard of the book, let alone read it, and given the current state of our educational system and the goals of our modern media, certainly neither can be presumed. The reason I say this may be obvi-ous to some and wholly baffling to others. It has to do with the fact that *1984* is possibly *too* relevant to our society now, and I could see why some might not want too many people going out of their way to read it.

I realize that I'm not the first person to see the parallel between "Newspeak" (the official language of the society described in the book, which was devised to meet the ideological needs of "the Party") and political correctness. The latter term is in fact an example of Orwell's Newspeak, in that it carries the presumption of truth in its contextual semantics.

The truth is that PC is a tool, well-devised to meet the ideological needs of the political left. In PC, as in Newspeak, things are not identified as they are, but rather with descriptors that more closely evoke the conceptualization the labelers would like us to have.

At first, as always, it was so insidious as to be benign, even humanitarian. Handicapped people became "challenged," despite the fact that they do in fact possess handicaps. Well, of course, everybody has sympathy for people with disabilities, right? Soon, illegal aliens became "undocumented workers" and genocide became "ethnic cleansing." Today, terrorists are "freedom fighters" or "insurgents" in the parlance of many in the press, and "tolerance" has come to mean acceptance of that which conflicts with the better judgment of most sound-minded people.

As it stands now, PC has infiltrated our domestic and foreign policy makers to a degree that is absolutely mind-boggling—as well as short-sighted, irresponsible, and collectively suicidal. Illegal aliens stream across our borders, and politicians ignore it, even over our objections, for fear of offending, though it has been established that terrorists and legions of violent criminals have entered the U.S. via our notoriously porous borders. Fringe groups and profiteers espouse and market perverse mind- and soul-stultifying bilge, yet it is ignored for fear of offending. As discussed here previously, it is quite literally part of the mechanism for keeping black Americans in a wretched state, and even with their tacit approval. Our leniency with Islamists, both at home and abroad, has been influenced by PC thought. Our enemies take advantage of it—as a weakness.

In *1984*, the Ministry of Truth (where the story's protagonist, Winston Smith, worked) used Newspeak to influence minds on a scale unheard of in 1949. Using Newspeak, they also employed an ancillary component thereof called Doublethink, a type of subtle mind manipulation. Using Doublethink, intimidation, and propaganda, the Party was able to condition people to accept the contradictions that emanated from the Ministry of Truth. The people came to believe that falsehoods were true, and that the Party was the only institution capable of distinguishing between right and wrong.

There is politically correct speech, of course, but there are also politically correct concepts; for example, the notion that illegal émigrés to the United States are entitled to certain rights—such as the right to be in the U.S. in the first place, among numerous others.

On the October 5, 2006, edition of Fox News's *The O'Reilly Factor*, host Bill O'Reilly excoriated Columbia University for some of their students' treatment of members of the Minuteman Project when they were invited there to speak by a campus Republican organization. The Minuteman Project is a citizen activist organization that addresses security issues concerning the U.S. Mexico border. Represented by video footage shown on O'Reilly's show, the Minutemen were heckled at Columbia in a most uncouth manner. This prompted O'Reilly to call for a suspension of all donations to the school by its alumni.

What I attempted to call attention to in a column I wrote following the incident was not so much the infantile and odious behavior of the Columbia students, but their treatment of Mr. O'Reilly's guest that night, who had been the first speaker at the event. Marvin Stewart, one of the members of the Minuteman Project, is a black man. During the interview with O'Reilly, Stewart related the story of having been subjected to an onslaught of racial epithets by the students, members of a socialist campus group that had somehow secreted themselves (and their signs and banners) in the auditorium.

The point I made then—which was a reiteration of that which I and others of varying ethnic backgrounds have asserted—is that the left, although they claim a monopoly on tolerance, are intolerant, hateful elites who prove themselves to be the real bigots time and again, despite their projection of these traits onto anyone who does not agree with them.

The Minuteman-Columbia incident was another example of blacks being "tolerated" by the left so long as they "keep their place." If they become a liability, or are so rash as to step out of line dogmatically, they are summarily shot from a cannon with all due alacrity—some may argue faster than a non-minority would be. All assertions to the contrary, the left expects minorities to be grateful and demure. Ironically, Stewart's harassment had its genesis in the PC view that illegal Mexican immigrants have some singular "right" to be present in the U.S. illegally. Like many beliefs concerning black Americans that have been extrapolated to their extreme, there is no rational basis for the latitude given to illegal immigrants from Mexico, Islamic émigrés, or other ethnic groups that always seem to represent the far left's nihilistic designs.

If we may briefly revisit the term "African-American" once more: The application and acceptance of this term—particularly among whites—was a case of negrophilia and political correctness having played off of one another, despite the former having come into being first. As with many aspects of race relations and race politics, no one wished to advance the idea that adopting a new idiom for referring to blacks was unnecessary and even ludicrous. It would not have been politically correct.

To illustrate how insidious these processes are, there are conservative whites who regularly make use of the term "African-American" despite the fact that their black conservative friends may refuse to do so. The reason for this is twofold; on an individual basis, it is usually a combination of these aspects. One is that said whites don't want the confrontation. Two is that it's not a conscious choice; its use has subtly crept into their lexicon.

For my part, I stand where I indicated earlier. I have no intention of parading around referring to myself as an African-German-Norwegian-English-Dutch–Native American–American in the name of all things politically correct.

It's *stupid.*

Most of these attitudes grew out of negrophiliac-inspired fallacies that presume and advance the idea that America—and more specifically, white Americans—have had a hand in all oppression of non-white people around the world. Similarly, the difficulties of just about all undeveloped nations can be uncannily traced either to imperialist or racist oppression by Americans; again, the inference is *by whites.*

THIRTEEN

negrophilia
and other ethnic minorities

T HIS CHAPTER WILL examine the effect of negrophilia on Americans' perception of and the political dynamics concerning other ethnic minorities. During the civil rights movement, some ethnic minorities other than blacks took advantage of the climate of reform—as well they should have—and sought to ameliorate some of the conditions and social injustice under which they suffered. Advances were made in these areas; however, many of the negative aspects of race politics and social dynamics that had their genesis in negrophilia wound up being extended to certain of these other ethnic groups. At present, there are some who barely have a leg to stand on vis-à-vis the subject of discrimination or institutional racism, who have simply jumped on the bandwagon of compulsory tolerance and political correctness; this includes ethnic and religious subgroups that actually have malicious agendas.

From World War II on, American Jews, the press, and the entertainment industry (within which happen to be many influential American Jews) had been acutely sensitive to anti-Semitism in America. The Holocaust was incomprehensibly horrific, yet the precedent for such atrocities in the modern West was wasted on many comfortable, post-

WWII Americans. Here, however, there were soldiers who had seen the death camps, as well as Jewish émigrés from Germany and Eastern Europe who still bore the scars and serial numbers on their forearms. They were among us, and not only determined that such a thing should never occur again, but resolute that all Americans remember what European and Russian Jews had suffered. *"Never again!"* was the cry of many American Jews, and many Jewish characters in the entertainment media.

For decades, since the establishment of Israel in 1948, an essential litmus test for national political candidates (as far as the majority of American Jews were concerned) was their stance on Israel. Unfortunately, due to the secularization of many American Jews and their alignment with the far left, there are those who essentially no longer identify themselves as Jewish. This has led to the baffling and dangerous phenomenon of their sympathizing with Islamic fascists, whom committed leftists support politically because doing so plays to their own nihilistic, anti-American sentiments. Among the secular bloc of Jewish voters that votes Democratic (there is a religious bloc that exists, and often votes Democratic as well) and the establishment press, there has been a marked change in allegiance since the 1970s, particularly in these bodies having incrementally withdrawn support for Israel. None of this, of course, would have any bearing on these American Jews being among the first to have their throats cut if said Muslim fanatics had their druthers.

In some ways, although Jews are technically a white minority and largely stood with blacks during the civil rights movement, they enjoyed (if you will) some of the benefits of negrophilia. Much of the confrontational sensitivity where the perception of racism was concerned on the part of Jews was understood and often accepted by the majority of Americans, because they had already come to empathize with the sufferings of blacks.

∞

Beginning in 1950, residents of the Caribbean island of Puerto Rico (a commonwealth of the U.S.) began to relocate to major cities in the

U.S., particularly New York City. As covered earlier, some sought better economic conditions in general, while others capitalized on the
broad criteria for public assistance.

It has long since been a standing joke that there are more Puerto
Ricans in New York than in Puerto Rico; in 2003, the U.S. Census
Bureau's estimates made that official. While there are Puerto Rican
communities in urban areas in which one might say the climate is
very "ethnic," for the most part, Puerto Ricans assimilated in much
the same way as did Italians, another non–English-speaking minority.
Interestingly, due to the colonially derived genotype in Puerto Rico
(which resembles that of Cuba), there are Puerto Ricans with blond
hair and blue eyes; there are also black Puerto Ricans, as well as the
majority who take on the *indio* ("Hispanic," in common, if inaccurate,
parlance) appearance.

Again, although Puerto Ricans faced less institutional racism than
blacks, some organized to ameliorate that which did exist. There were
some protests in the late 1960s, and labor-related movements, as well
as more militant types, such as the former Young Lords in Spanish
Harlem in New York.

In 1974, Fuerzas Armadas de Liberación Nacional (FALN), a Puerto
Rican terrorist group that advocated independence for Puerto Rico,
began a bombing campaign in the U.S. (mostly in large cities with a
sizeable Puerto Rican contingent) that lasted through 1984. Their
aim was to establish a Marxist-Leninist government on the island, à
la Cuba.

Their modus operandi was to set off explosive devices in public
places, sometimes several in a series, and leave behind communiqués
with their demands. While the idea of a political organization demand-
ing independence for Puerto Rico may leave the reader in stitches, all
in all, they were responsible for more than one hundred and twenty
bombings. The number of FALN members who were maimed by bombs
that went off prematurely rivaled that of their victims.

Lack of public support for the FALN (as well as hardly any among
Puerto Ricans at large) is indicative of why many Americans have never
heard of them, but in August of 1999, President Clinton commuted

the sentences of sixteen FALN members, no doubt titillating those on the left. While most political and apolitical Puerto Ricans have mainstreamed, in recent years, more from the Puerto Rican community have aligned themselves with generic leftist Latino activist organizations such as the National Council of La Raza (NCLR). One example is the recently appointed Supreme Court Justice Sonia Sotomayor, who was a long-standing member of La Raza, despite its primary function being that of advocating for illegal immigrants from Mexico.

The controversial nature of Sotomayor's appointment was a poignant example of negrophilia in action on a few levels; racist comments she had uttered, a particular decision she had made that many considered racist, and her stated affinity for affirmative action were among the primary reasons her detractors were detractors to start with.

∽

In the case of Americans of Mexican descent, and Mexicans in the U.S. illegally, here, there are much more sinister designs at work than negrophilia, ones that involve all manner of bureaucratic, corporate, and political chicanery. In my 2007 book, *Annexing Mexico: Solving the Border Problem through Annexation and Assimilation*, I went into great detail concerning that of which many Americans are aware as regards illegal Mexican émigrés to the U.S.: the corruption in government (on both sides of the border), abominable ethics in business, and weak border management that fuel illegal immigration. An exhaustive reprise of same is not essential here.

As negrophilia and the attendant obliging schools of thought took hold in America, the idea that the United States somehow owed Mexican immigrants access to employment, health care, and ancillary benefits of living in America became increasingly prevalent. Organizations such as the National Council of La Raza and Fuerza Latina lobbied for laws (such as sanctuary city laws) that facilitated illegal immigration, and much for the same reason that blacks blindly follow black politicians and activists (misplaced ethnic pride), Americans of Mexican descent support these efforts despite the deleterious effects illegal immigration has on all American citizens, Latinos included.

Still, there is a great deal more at work here than an upsurge in the public's sympathy for poor Mexicans, many of whom are actually fleeing racist practices and policies in Mexico. Public outrage over the damage done to areas of the Southwest and its economy would be greater save for the cries of racism that rise whenever citizens or politicians press border issues. The above modus operandi is simply negrophilia, moved laterally to address another progressive objective: the conscription of Latino émigrés into the far-left fold.

∽

Probably, the most immediately dangerous manifestation of negro-philia today (again, laterally transposed to another ethnic minority) is America's equivocation regarding those of Arabic, Indo-European, and Asian descent who practice the Islamic religion. It is also a stellar example of the extraordinary imprudence (some would say insanity) that Americans are becoming accustomed to practicing vis-à-vis groups with whom we have "issues;" these used to be known as "enemies."

It is my personal view, as well as that of many Muslim converts to Christianity, that Islam is wholly incompatible with Western society. Although there is some disagreement on the semantics, the nearest translation for "Islam" is "submission" or "to submit." Islam is the most naturally xenophobic of all the religions that came out of the Middle East; while there are certain tenets of that religion that appear quite moral and honorable, the idea that Islam must ultimately hold pre-eminence on Earth is thoroughly ingrained into Muslim doctrine.

Thus, it becomes inevitable that when a Muslim community—regardless of how peaceful or industrious it had been—reaches that elusive, unquantifiable critical mass in a non-Muslim society, factions within that community will attempt to subjugate that society. Non-militant Muslims will acquiesce for reasons of faith or fear, and do nothing to stop it. This is precisely what we are seeing in much of the West pertaining to the dynamic between assimilated Muslims and jihadists.

Negrophilia, inasmuch as it paved the way for political correctness, has been one of the weapons used to beat the American conscience into submission. At this juncture, progressives appear perfectly willing to accept and promote the aspect of radical Muslim dogma, which holds that the West (and, by extension, America) has behaved criminally in its relations with the Muslim world, and therefore owes restitution, even if that means cheerfully baring our throats so that they might be slit.

Though it is manifestly insane that Americans should give political latitude to a faction (either within our borders or without) that has vowed to conquer and/or kill us, progressives have advanced and attempted to justify this idea. Given the allegiance that they hold for the far left, the solidarity they have been directed to feel for radical Islam, and the admonitions of prominent American black Muslims, many blacks in America can also be counted among those sympathetic to radical Islam.

FOURTEEN

negrophilia
in public education

T HE CLOSER ONE gets to a fire, the more one feels the heat. The closer one gets to a fresh pile of dog crap, the worse the stink. And the closer one gets to any major urban center in America, the more intensely one will experience the influence of the political left. Government is proportionally much bigger there than in other areas. Taxes and the cost of living are higher. Corruption in government is often rampant. The use of toll roads is widespread. Gun control is tight. The number of stultified civil liberties and inane little citations one might face as a business owner, homeowner, landlord, or even the operator of a motor vehicle—all of which result in fines—increase to ridiculous proportions.

And, of course, the quality of education in public schools plummets.

As we know, the major urban centers are where the majority of black Americans dwell. I shouldn't have to include a history lesson on the education of black Americans; it's not to be condescending, I swear. For most readers of this book, it probably isn't necessary. Still, as time goes by, there is an increasing number of Americans who have never been sufficiently apprised of what used to be considered basic truths apropos any given subject, or significant historical events, that many of us assume "everybody" knows.

The experience of blacks in the public school system is a microcosm of the overall experience of Americans at large; it is also a potent example thereof. Given our current course, we have perhaps ten or twenty years before the social engineering going on in public schools and universities has Americans so dumbed-down that there will be nothing but a fringe minority left to protest the onslaught of encroaching socialist measures. When citizens or commentators criticize socialistic or communistic measures being proposed by government (as occurred with health care reform in 2009), their impact will be minimal. When one examines outcomes for blacks and education, one observes the result progressives in government would like to see pertaining to all Americans.

Author David Horowitz's 1997 book *Radical Son: A Generational Odyssey,* provides one of the most insightful forays into the educational system in America. Horowitz is the child of two Jewish communist teachers from New York City. Raised to be a communist, Horowitz reports in his book that an overwhelming majority of administrators and teachers in the New York City public school system in the fifties and sixties were card-carrying communists. A widely accepted protocol for communists around the globe, these cells conspired to indoctrinate school children with leftist sensibilities incrementally, at as early an age as possible. They started with New York.

As I have written previously in my columns, the model for the modern public school system in America has been incrementally modified after that which emerged in New York ever since. Individuals within the administrative structure often went on to occupy positions in the state and federal government. Al Shanker, a legendary figure within the teaching community in New York, and a decidedly far-left character, was president of the United Federation of Teachers from 1964 to 1984, and president of the American Federation of Teachers from 1974 to 1997. These unions have held to the progressive philosophy, and are responsible for the intractability of progressivism and professional mediocrity within America's public schools. *All* of the moral ambivalence and social engineering we see emerging in America starts here. Shanker helped to hone the aforementioned educational model, and went on to become an "educational advisor" to presidents George H. W. Bush and Bill Clinton.

When discussing black schools or the education of blacks, more often than not what is primarily being addressed are kindergarten-through-twelfth grade schools, and the quality of education in urban areas in which blacks predominate. Generally, these are referred to as "inner-city" schools.

"Though widely known failures in the eyes of Americans across the political spectrum, black inner-city schools have been a great success from the perspective of what Washington officials and progressive lawmakers have been striving to make them for the last four decades.

"The dropout rate for black youth reached an historic low of 11% in 2005."[7] In 1972 it was 21 percent. Here's the sick part: "This drop is at least in part related to increased incarceration rates among black male high school dropouts, which more than doubled between 1980 and 1999, thus removing them from the civilian non-institutionalized population on which these estimates are based."[8] So, among those black youth who are not dropping out of school per se, the reason lies in that they are going to jail or prison.

While the gap between whites and blacks in academic attainment and achievement has narrowed over the last few decades, the percentages of black school children in impoverished households and those headed by single females have increased. Although the overall number of blacks in poverty has decreased, the percentages of blacks in poverty remain inordinately high. As a consequence, the number of black students who fall through the cracks, winding up unable to earn a living wage, or turning to crime, is considered to be at crisis levels.

So, more than 11 percent never finish high school; of those who go on to college, in most instances, one can presume that (after being raised in inner cities, with their attendant high concentration of progressives, cult of resentment, and exposure to subversive sentiments) these wind up at state universities and develop the archetypal progressive mind-set. They're inordinately critical of our system of government and capitalism, and blame a cabal of nonexistent, wealthy white men for the wretchedness they barely escaped.

It's a win-win proposition for progressives, though a highly questionable deal for blacks.

My first encounter with social engineering and incompetence within the school system—at least, the first I can recall—came when I was in the first month or so of grade school. I began attending public schools in New York in the 1960s, where many of the institutions and practices red state folks fear today were already well in place. I'll clarify: When I first heard the phrase "political correctness," my reaction was one of recognition rather than perplexity; they'd finally found a name for it. The analogy to Orwell's Newspeak was definitely not lost on me.

I was oblivious to what was occurring at the time, of course, but here's what happened: I was pulled from my class and placed in one of less than a dozen children. I was puzzled, but I was only six, so I went where, and did what, I was told. The kids in this class were ones I recalled having seen before, but never in a regular classroom setting. I recall that none of them communicated particularly well, to put it politely.

To put it impolitely, I had been placed in a class of children who were one step away from the local home for the mentally retarded. The school had not yet finished determining if these kids, with an assortment of speech impediments, behavioral anomalies, and yet-undiagnosed learning disabilities, were going to be able to assimilate into the mainstream academic environment or would need to be transferred to a facility more appropriately equipped to educate them, such as it was.

At this point the reader might be wondering how a mental defective such as myself managed to overcome some terribly limiting handicap, particularly during that juncture in our history, and ultimately develop into someone who can put more than a few words together at a time.

In all humility, there really wasn't that much to overcome. You see, a few weeks prior to the beginning of school that year, I had lost one of my front teeth; consequently, I had a very pronounced lisp. The enlightened, sensitive educational professionals into whose charge I had been placed quickly surmised that I was probably retarded and off I went. No official notice was given to me or my parents.

When my parents discovered this horrible (but oh so characteristic) blunder, they were understandably infuriated, and demanded I be returned to my class. The properly chagrined school administrators clumsily complied. These days, my family would likely have netted an easy few million in the civil settlement behind this unfortunate occurrence. Emotional distress, you know . . .

Later in my grade school career, I experienced being whisked off to the school psychologist's office and Rorschached (inkblot-tested) on more than one occasion for such things as cursing out a bully as he physically assaulted me.

"Do you realize that you could have permanently damaged his psyche?" queried the horrified administrators. On other occasions, after tangling with black kids (for the record, I tangled with white ones, too), I was admonished by administrators to try to "understand" these kids' frustrations and feelings; you see, unlike them, *I* had a father who was living at home, and worse—*he was white.*

I have stated before that my disdain for the political left comes not from some insular, moralistic intellectualism; I've lived in the belly of the beast and experienced the spirit-killing judgment and smug, cavalier self-assuredness of those for whom bureaucracy itself has become the chief arbiter of wisdom. The well-intentioned have simply been deceived, but the power brokers are manifestly evil. These are the attitudes and the ineptitude with which the political left has offhandedly consigned millions of black students to mediocrity, and worse.

I speak from authority, not because I consider myself the chief arbiter of wisdom, but because the childhood scenarios described above, and subsequent ones, have illustrated for me too plainly that the socialistic machine some hoped would one day displace our current system—despite having wrought nothing but degradation and ruin in the nations which employed it—is malevolent by nature.

Yet, the aforementioned power brokers continue to deftly incite their acolytes and the well-intentioned into divisive thought and action using such vile creatures as Ward Churchill and Helen Caldecott, who travel the country claiming that we are a fascist nation, and columnist DeWayne Wickham, who said that the 2004 national election was an instance of the white man attempting to "take back power."

From whom, I couldn't say. "The people," perhaps, is how it usually goes, and "the people" are forever galvanized in their "struggle" against "the Man," or some comparable sinister, faceless enemy. It's worked pretty well for Castro, as it did in the Soviet Union for eighty years.

The eternal secret, cloaked in the big lie, of course—which I discovered in grade school—is that, for them, the real enemy is *us.*

I believe that the preceding examples illustrate a level of detachment and incompetence on the part of public education that is exponentially multiplied in the education of black students. I do not assert that blacks are the only ones who suffer from this syndrome; the protocol is essentially the same in more rural areas. It was, I suppose, perversely serendipitous for progressives, who controlled education in urban areas, that they had this opportunity to have a crack at so many black students.

On the syllabus side, since negrophilia is a device of the political left, and this bloc controls the public educational system, the indoctrination of students of every race is essential. A key element, in addition to decrying the evil and injustice of America's founders, our Republic, and capitalism, is promoting the idea that other cultures and societies are more good and just.

One manifestation of this is the idea that certain tribal societies, and pre-Columbian peoples in particular, had it *so much more "together"* than modern Westerners. They are often portrayed as more righteous, moral, and munificent than Westerners (particularly during North America's colonial period) could ever hope to be. They respected nature, each other, and were generally more benevolent all around than we are—and our evil forebears went and bred them out of existence, or killed them. This notion is also promoted vigorously and insidiously by the entertainment media, in the form of educational programming and documentaries.

While it has been acknowledged here that Northern Europeans did commit atrocities galore in their colonization of the Americas, it is also undeniable that their actions were no different from those of other ascendant societies throughout history. It is quite true that some of these tribal societies possessed remarkable development in particular areas, such as art, architecture, and science, often far beyond what was once believed. Some were far more attuned to the natural world than their conquerors were, or than their descendants came to be, and held to some practices that were more prudent and conservative than that of many modern societies.

To advance the idea that these societies were somehow superior to ours, however, is patent silliness, as well as propagandistic. Most were indeed primitive with respect to their conquerors' standards, and also implemented practices that were considered barbaric, such as human sacrifice. Modern historians from tribal backgrounds are often the first to admit that European colonialists (not all of whom were white) often employed the same sort of warfare and subjugation with which tribal societies were accustomed. It is only the influence of twentieth-century white progressives that gave rise to their practice of whining about the injustice of it all. You don't hear Irish people complaining about the red hair they inherited from Vikings who invaded Ireland centuries ago . . .

FIFTEEN

negrophilia
and the economy

T HIS CHAPTER MIGHT never have been written, if not for one event described herein.

Why? For a few reasons. One is that, although this book could easily have been a scholarly study with pages of footnotes and hundreds more insights and anecdotes, most readers of sociopolitical commentary, including myself, simply don't want to read a thousand-page book. This could have been a *long* book. Too long, in fact. Making the points herein simply does not require that much time or space. If you decide that you'd like to hear more, by all means, let me know.

The main reason I almost did not address negrophilia as it relates to the economy is this: For the most part, all save for the rich and powerful in America are in the same boat as far as the economy goes. Usually, it's the middle class that gets hit the hardest during tough economic times, regardless of race. In America, people below the poverty line (which includes poor black Americans) actually don't feel the effect of economic downturns as much as other Americans do, because their so-called advocates in government act as a buffer between them and adversity. After all, that's part of the arrangement: Should these "advocates" not come through consistently, they lose their political power. So, the entitlements keep coming, regardless of what happens to be going on with the economy. You and I might go broke and lose our retirements and homes (along with untold numbers of other working Americans), but those receiving entitlements never lose a thing.

Still, that isn't something that's restricted to poor black people, so I might not have brought it up.

The waste resulting in the exploitation of black Americans by political factions—that is, the productivity lost due to so many being kept down—is definitely a collective moral failing on the part of our nation, and more so because blacks were exploited for so long in other ways. Obviously, when any group is exploited to their detriment, unable to realize their fullest potential and contribute in commensurate measure, the economy—and the nation overall—suffers.

But black Americans are not the only group that fails to reach its full potential due to the interference of politicians, activists, and government. So, again, I might not have addressed this subject respecting the economy.

But then, *something happened* . . .

That which precipitated my decision to include this chapter is not only one of the most severe and extreme manifestations of negrophilia to date, but became one of the most harmful occurrences to impinge on the U.S. economy in its history, and subsequently, the American people, save for past military conflicts in which we have become engaged.

The Community Reinvestment Act (CRA) was a federal law passed in 1977 (during the Carter administration). Ostensibly, it was calculated to promote the accommodation of mortgage borrowers across socioeconomic lines on the part of the banking community. One of the concerns being addressed at the time, according to Congress, was a discriminatory credit practice against low-income and minority communities called "redlining," wherein lenders avoided lending in low-income (and, consequently, some minority) communities because they were considered bad risks.

Leaving aside the fact that minorities of good financial standing have

always been able to secure housing, and that it is a sound economic practice to lend to such people regardless of their race, and an unsound practice to lend to people of poor creditworthiness regardless of their race,
Congress claimed that it had grounds for this action.

Or so they said . . .

The CRA was enforced by federal regulatory agencies, which
regularly examined banking institutions for compliance, *and federal
approval and cooperation when it came to lenders' applications for expansions
and acquisitions was predicated upon adherence to the CRA on the part of
lenders.*

During the Bill Clinton and George W. Bush administrations, the
scope of the CRA was widened, and funding through lenders became
increasingly more accessible. All of this was sold to the public—those
few who were paying attention—as helping Americans (read *black*
Americans) to actualize "the dream of home ownership," but effectively amounted to affirmative action loans to the uncreditworthy. As
usual, no one was going to stand in the way of black Americans getting
what was coming to them, and there was no way the average American
could possibly have known what was ahead. The few economists who
could see the potential for disaster were ignored.

Much of the impetus behind this increased employment of the
Community Reinvestment Act was due to the efforts of certain "community organizations" that began putting massive amounts of political
pressure on members of Congress, the Clinton and Bush administrations, and mortgage lenders. Using federal review, lawsuits, protests,
and threats of boycotts, these organizations essentially bullied lenders
into surrendering billions of dollars for use in high-risk loans.

Two of these "community organizations" were the Neighborhood
Assistance Corporation of America (NACA) and the Association of
Community Organizations for Reform Now (ACORN). "In the 1980s,
groups such as the activists at ACORN began pushing charges of
'redlining'—claims that banks discriminated against minorities in
mortgage lending."[9]

This, of course, would have been in violation of the Community
Reinvestment Act, thus eliciting compliance on the part of lenders.

*ACORN is the nation's largest grassroots community organization of
low- and moderate-income people with over 400,000 member families
organized into more than 1,200 neighborhood chapters in about 75
cities across the country. Since 1970, ACORN has been building
community organizations that are committed to social and economic
justice, and won victories on thousands of issues of concern to our
members, through direct action, negotiation, legislative advocacy and
voter participation. ACORN helps those who have historically been
locked out become powerful players in our democratic system.*
—From ACORN's Web site

Now, ACORN was (and, at the time of this writing, still is) essentially a criminal enterprise. Despite receiving more than $50 million in federal funds since 1994, they have exercised a partisan agenda, pursued ineligible individuals with the intent of registering them to vote, and knowingly registered thousands of parties to vote multiple times. ACORN workers have been convicted of submitting false voter registration forms in numerous states; fully one-third of the 1.3 million voter registration cards turned in by ACORN in 2008 wound up being bogus. By way of damage control, ACORN brass tried to defray criticism by claiming that the first few instances of this were errant workers acting on their own.

As the incidents racked up, however, their affirmations that these exceptional and infrequent crimes were committed by "rogue" employees became less and less believable.

*Operationally, ACORN is a shell game played in 120 cities,
43 states and the District of Columbia through a complex structure
designed to conceal illegal activities, to use taxpayer and tax-exempt
dollars for partisan political purposes, and to distract investigators.
Structurally, ACORN is a chess game in which senior management is
shielded from accountability by multiple layers of volunteers
and compensated employees who serve as pawns to take the fall
for every bad act.*
—STAFF REPORT, U.S. House of Representatives, Committee on
Oversight and Government Reform, July 23, 2009

In the late summer of 2009, video footage began to surface in the press, produced by twenty-five-year-old filmmaker James O'Keefe and his partner, Hannah Giles, a twenty-year-old student. Through undercover work, they were able to very effectively implicate ACORN in providing counseling to Giles and O'Keefe (who were posing as a prostitute and her pimp, respectively) that amounted to criminal conspiracy. These recordings took place in several U.S. cities, and consisted of ACORN workers and legal advisors counseling Giles and O'Keefe in everything from tax evasion to establishing houses of prostitution in which underage illegal immigrant girls would be employed.

It suddenly became apparent to millions of Americans (as opposed to the handful of us "fringe racists" who patronize the "right wing hate press") that ACORN stank to high heaven. Even the casual observer could now clearly see that ACORN drew its policies and its workers from the gutter (in the case of the latter, perhaps quite literally), and that nefarious modes and methods were far more likely to have been endemic to the organization than its executives argued.

And did you notice the use of the phrase "social and economic justice" in the excerpt from ACORN's Web site? Yes—the mating call of the Marxist. And speaking of Marxists, who of all people was revealed to have had deep and long-standing ties to ACORN? President Barack Obama; he brought them on board in various advisory and administrative capacities when he took office as president. Obama formerly provided them with legal representation and taught classes for them, and they endorsed his 2008 presidential campaign. This, of course, gives rise to the question of how much ACORN learned from Obama, given that he instructed their operatives.

Finally, even a Congress eyeballs-deep in the mess could no longer ignore the danger ACORN represented to its credibility, even among its political base.

Specifically, the report by the House Committee on Oversight and Government Reform from July of 2009 made the following criminal allegations:

First, ACORN has evaded taxes, obstructed justice, engaged in self-dealing, and aided and abetted a cover-up of embezzlement by Dale Rathke, the brother of ACORN founder Wade Rathke. . . .

Second, ACORN has committed investment fraud, deprived the public of its right to honest services, and engaged in racketeering affecting interstate commerce. . . .

Third, ACORN has committed a conspiracy to defraud the United States by using taxpayer funds for partisan political activities. . . .

Fourth, ACORN has submitted false filings to the Internal Revenue Service (IRS) and the Department of Labor, in addition to violating the Fair Labor Standards Act (FLSA). . . .

Fifth, ACORN falsified and concealed facts concerning an illegal transaction between related parties in violation of the Employee Retirement Income Security Act of 1974 (ERISA). . . .

ACORN'S RADICAL SOCIALIST ORIGINS

ACORN owes its origin to a revolutionary strategy developed in the 1960s by Columbia University's professor of social work Richard A. Cloward and his research associate, Frances Fox Piven.

In what became known as the Cloward-Piven strategy, the two sociologists argued for a revolutionary approach to mobilizing the poor. They advocated a form of class warfare against capitalist forces perceived as exploiters of labor and oppressors of the poor.

David Horowitz, a longtime student of leftist political movements in the United States, characterized the Cloward-Piven strategy as seeking "to hasten the fall of capitalism by overloading the government bureaucracy with a flood of impossible demands, thus pushing society into crisis and economic collapse."

Cloward and Piven argued a "guaranteed annual income" should be established as an entitlement for the poor.

Arguing for massive registration of the poor in existing social welfare programs, Cloward and Piven sought to create a crisis that could be exploited to obtain a fundamental redistribution of power in favor of the "have-nots."

Advancing their socialist revolutionary aims, Cloward and Piven explained the crisis they sought "can occur spontaneously (e.g., riots) or as the intended result of tactics of demonstration and protest which either generate institutional disruption or bring unrecognized disruption to public attention."

The Cloward-Piven strategy sought to apply the tactics of the revolutionary civil-rights movement, including urban riots, to the poor as a whole, transcending interest-group politics defined by race to involve interest group politics defined by class.[10]

In the case of subprime mortgages obtained via machinations of the CRA, the aforementioned uncreditworthy Americans defaulted by the millions, then mortgage-backed securities collapsed, resulting in the economic crisis whose tsunami-like waves reached around the globe. It's that simple.

Some in Congress, and others in government, promoted and acted under the auspices of the Community Reinvestment Act, so part of the responsibility for this fiasco rests squarely in their laps. These largely congressional Democrats include Senator Christopher J. Dodd (D-CT) and Congressman Barney Frank (D-MA); they continue—occasionally with marked belligerence—to defend their actions and failed institutions such as government-sponsored mortgage "brokers" Fannie Mae and Freddie Mac, when such comportment is indefensible, *quod erat demonstrandum.*

What validates the claim that all this was an instance of negrophilia is threefold:

1. If the Community Reinvestment Act was ostensibly benign (here we'll assume for the sake of argument that it was), its imprudent widening under Clinton and Bush was still in response to political pressure from far-left minority activists.
2. The CRA could not have been sold to the American people

unless they had been thoroughly propagandized with negro-philiac sensibilities.

3. Had the American people *not* been propagandized with negrophiliac sensibilities, ACORN and NACA wouldn't have had a leg to stand on vis-à-vis intimidating mortgage lenders or their public relations departments. Had lenders perceived these organizations as not having public support, they would have told ACORN and NACA to go screw themselves.

As previously mentioned, ACORN was founded by Wade Rathke, a creature of the farthest left. In his youth during the 1960s, he was dedicatedly active in "welfare rights" organizations; these were Marxist groups that ostensibly were geared to ensuring that people on public assistance were receiving their maximum allowed benefits. Their real purpose, however, was to enroll as many people as possible on public assistance, exact as much in the way of benefits as possible, and collapse America's economy. This is not an accusation; their principals readily admitted to this fact.

This is what ACORN was created to accomplish—and it just might have succeeded, except that the coup de grâce was via the housing market, rather than directly through entitlement programs. Though ACORN's efforts, utilizing the Community Reinvestment Act, were promoted as altruistic, their goal—their stated goal—has *always* been the devastation of the American economy, which would necessitate "emergency" government intervention.

Then, at precisely the right moment, a Marxist who was in league with ACORN *just happened* to get elected president of the United States.

How uncanny . . .

The "big, bad suits" involved—whom much of America has been brainwashed by Congress and the establishment press into blaming solely for the crisis—were executives in the private sector who took gargantuan bonuses and golden parachutes while the stock market induced motion sickness. Largely, they remained unassailable, save for harsh (albeit disingenuous) criticism from news organizations and lawmakers. In a way, this was only fair; no one else who bore responsibility—the activists, senators, and congressmen—were held accountable either. The lenders and Wall Street execs were the fall guys; they got to skate with their millions (in some cases, billions) as long as the left could pin the entire debacle on them in the eyes of the American people.

The reason this was allowed is that no one in government wished to do much more than scratch the surface, lest their complicity be revealed. In some cases, though the press was mum on this fact, the necessity for lawmakers to keep their part in it under wraps rested with the fact that they received campaign donations from Fannie and Freddie. This includes President (then Senator) Barack Obama, *the largest recipient of these donations behind Dodd*, who received the most.

I want to own a Maybach Exelero. This luxury supercar currently boasts a sticker price of eight million dollars. I could probably count on one hand the number of Americans who own one. Statistically speaking, even if I become a millionaire, I won't be able to afford a Maybach Exelero.

And that ticks me off. I deserve one, don't I? I can appreciate quality things as well as the next guy, can't I?

So, should the world economy be forced to implode on the account of everyone who might be willing to stand in line behind self-serving "community organizations" that plan to bully the auto industry and government agencies into arranging that each of us receive a Maybach? That question scarcely merits an answer, of course. People without means don't get what they can't afford, whether it be Kobe beef steaks, supercars, or houses. That's the way things work in the real world; Marxist utopian fantasies don't count, because they're false visions in which no one but the silver-tongued leadership gets what they want. At this point, such fare appeals only to those who have been propagandized beyond the point of redemption, and the naturally dim.

But that ridiculous supercar scenario is *precisely* what happened regarding the Community Reinvestment Act, activist organizations such as ACORN, and complicity among lenders and lawmakers such as Frank, Dodd, and Obama. You may be suffering at this very moment so that fools could buy houses they couldn't afford to pay for, and so that those parties could further solidify their political power and amass personal wealth.

I could triumphantly declare that it was all negrophilia, my pet beef and that which I am now revealing to the world with a grand flourish, that caused the global economic crisis that reared its head in the fall of 2008, but that would be disingenuous. It was a *combination* of negrophilia, self-seeking activists, crooked politicians, and corporate greed that brought it on. But the catalyst was the effort of well-organized far-left activists, ostensibly acting on the behalf of black Americans—and no one in power in America was prepared to deny blacks their monstrously ill-placed "due" because they were afraid of getting shredded in the press. The result? A *global* financial catastrophe.

Is that sick, or *what?*

SIXTEEN

do the right thing

Conversation Piece: *It seems like [fill in activist's name] has done pretty well for himself/herself. So, remind me: just what is it that he/she has done for underprivileged black Americans?*

"Don't take it personally," I tell black people when one finally figures it out, and he or she is angry. "They want to make slaves of us all."

We currently have a situation in which 90 percent of black Americans are politically aligned with that which is profoundly evil, people and forces that are poised to transform our society into something wholly other, the antithesis of its intention, and something with which, when completed, Americans will not be pleased. By then, however, it will be far too late. Additionally, a substantial segment of our population has been intimidated into abject fear of criticizing or opposing black Americans and their so-called benefactors and allies. Thus, such would-be critics have been effectively neutralized as agents of our nation's preservation.

That so many blacks are aligned with these people and these forces is an extraordinarily dangerous thing. Should circumstances get truly unpleasant with hostilities between those Americans who are becoming increasingly frustrated, angry, and afraid at the prospect of losing their country and their liberties, and those aligned with the people who seek to take them, blacks will make easily distinguishable targets. This concerns me.

Events have been developing very rapidly since January of 2009; where we will be, particularly regarding the Obama presidency, by the time this book goes to press, remains to be seen. It is very troubling that while this administration may prove to be the most harmful to this nation, no one wants America's first black president to be left with a tarnished legacy. Hence, I believe that many deleterious policies advanced by this president will be tolerated, to our peril.

Young black fools spew about racism, when they don't have a clue as to what racism really is in practice; they've never experienced discrimination, bigotry, or felt the sting of institutional racism. Race-baiters continue to intimate that, under the surface, most whites are big, fat racists, and Americans cannot publicly cite their dishonesty, hypersensitivity, and compulsive diatribes, or they're called even bigger, fatter racists!

Conversation Piece: *So, why do you think it is that, for the last fifty years, black people have been voting for the party that supported slavery and segregation?*

The political left has attempted to characterize all who oppose President Obama's policies as fringe elements and racists. These are among the most craven, loathsome exertions I have ever witnessed. Yet, those who insist upon playing the race card do so with impunity, since the only ones around who criticize such action have been "the right wing hate press" and fringe racists.

Perhaps we can change that . . .

Prior to his spiritual awakening (after which he became markedly less militant and anti-American), the late civil-rights activist Malcolm X referred to blacks who believed they could ultimately thrive within the American system as "house niggers," analogizing them to blacks in the slave era who lived with the master in the house, supposedly had a greater affinity for him, and were more amenable to subservience. As I have done in the past, here I analogize modern black activists and progressive black politicians who adhere to the predominant far-left paradigm as *foremen*. During slavery, the foreman was the slave who worked under the overseer, a white employee of the owner. The overseer was the one who drove the field hands (or "field niggers") and meted out punishment. If the field hands weren't cutting it, or if someone misbehaved, the foreman got the worst of it. It was the foreman who held the unenviable position of having to betray other slaves, and he was often maligned and ostracized. Today, black activists and politicians play foremen to white progressive overseers, ensuring that other blacks stay in line.

What can be done to neutralize negrophilia? I've given clues throughout the course of this book; one was the practice for dealing with racists proscribed by my parents (and, no doubt, other people's parents) when I was a child: As far as possible within reason, *simply have nothing to do with them.* In some cases, this may be more difficult than in others, but it's not impossible; I once had to stay in a job with a bigoted individual—a white man who had no qualms about calling me a nigger right to my face—until I could find another job, because I needed the money. It didn't take long.

Legislation did not aid in eradicating racism or bigotry in America; the conscience of Americans did. All legislation (which reflected the Americans' beliefs) did, was to make institutional racism more difficult to practice. From 1955 to 1965, the worldview of many Americans changed dramatically. Only when people began to openly and unequivocally eschew racists and racist practices did things begin to transform. Only when others began to realize that practicing racism was going to make it difficult for them to maintain employment, do business, and cultivate relationships of all types were they persuaded to take a long, hard look at their belief systems.

Conversation Piece: *Did you know that it was the Republican Party that backed the Civil Rights Act of 1964? Yeah, the Democrats tried to vote it down . . .*

The second stratagem I would advance is that of *speaking the truth.* Ostracizing those who practice negrophilia and other forms of what some would call "reverse racism" will take courage. In some circles, we are the ones who will be ostracized. It will be difficult for whites to declare to their propagandized friends, family, and co-workers that white guilt is a sham; many will face reactions similar to that which they might face if they claimed the Holocaust did not occur.

It will take guts for black Americans to stand up to brainwashed blacks and assert that Brother Jesse and Brother Al are worse than the "house niggers" Malcolm X used to harp on, worse because no one is holding a whip or the threat of death over them. It has taken me a long time to cultivate the unyielding conviction that the opinions of those who cast the sort of invective used in the foreword of this book are as invalid as those of the white segregationists who used to stand on sidewalks alongside Civil Rights Movement marches and hurl racial epithets at the participants.

If you're white, you know damn well whether or not you're a racist. Racism isn't, as über-progressives might suggest, some insidious, latent psychological trait, like the repressed memories of some trauma. You have the ability to ask yourself whether or not you're sufficiently sensitive to those valid concerns of your fellow Americans who belong to ethnic minorities. You're also able to determine whether or not you've been intimidated or your speech stultified by concerns over how others might react to it. If we are going to stem the tide of this dangerous trend, it may be time for you to consider speaking that aforementioned truth. You don't have to become an activist, but, armed with facts, you have a better chance of enlightening your neighbors and winning hearts and minds if you speak, rather than stay silent. Much of the ammunition you need is right here in this book.

If you're not white, you can ask yourself the same questions. You also might ask yourself whether you, or anyone you know, might have fallen prey to some of the harmful methods and attitudes contained herein, the ones that have conspired to hamstring the economic, social, and spiritual growth of blacks (and other non-white ethnic minorities) under the guise of helping them. Can you, in good conscience, really justify the fifty years of failure that progressive politicians and activists offer, while they become wealthy and powerful, and blacks and browns continue to founder? Can you, in good conscience, advocate continuing on that same path?

Ask yourself this as well: Do you consider yourself an American, or do you consider yourself something else? Do you see yourself as sharing the same destiny as your neighbors, regardless of race, and do you envision a truly color-blind society, or do you look at your white neighbors as threats and enemies? Are you someone who really wants to see the vision of Rev. Dr. Martin Luther King Jr. come to fruition? Would you be surprised to know that in the hearts and minds of most Americans, it has already happened?

If you consider yourself something other than American, if you still believe that America is an institutionally racist nation, and if what I propose still seems like heresy, then you're probably best served right behind the progressives, socialists, and Marxists who have shepherded black Americans for the last forty years. Go right on working with them, and hope for the dawn of a new nation, one in which all of the things they have promised you, your parents, and your grandparents, might one day come true. Who knows—perhaps, someday, you'll even get to see some white man arrested for refusing to move to the back of the bus.

Regardless of your ethnic background, if we're on the same page (or if you suspect that we might be shortly) as far as what I offer here, I hope that this book provides you with some intelligent starting points for discussions with your fellows and fellowettes—such as the "Conversation Pieces" placed throughout this chapter.

Conversation Piece: *Did you ever hear about the "Klanbake"? Oh, boy—let me tell you about it . . . [Details in Chapter Four]*

Do not bother trying to convert your über-lib friends, if you have any. It will only depress you. If someone is oh-so-confident, arrogant, or even belligerent in their views, and definitely *has their rap down*, just leave them alone. Black folks, for example, who use such phraseology as "Ya see, the *white* man . . ." are *not* people who can reasonably be expected to come around. Neither are profoundly guilty-feeling white progressives. I have had some painful experiences with people who were very intelligent—some of whom had even been dear friends—who were simply too indoctrinated to approach. In some instances, it was akin to the archetypical *hometown boy meets childhood sweetheart years later* literary device; hometown boy discovers to his horror that childhood sweetheart is now a hardened, junkie whore, with the worldview of . . . well, a hardened, junkie whore. It's heartbreaking and, frankly, more than a little creepy.

I would advise not giving people too much credit for rationality just because they are of above-average intelligence. That can get you into a lot of trouble. Don't expect someone to listen to reason simply because they're well-educated, either. Some of these folks are among the worst adherents to progressive dogma. The more education some people have, the more likely they are to have their egos wrapped up in their convictions, however irrational. You threaten their egos, and their emotions spring forward with a vengeance. If they have a master's degree (it doesn't matter in what area—it could be javelin catching), and you have a bachelor's, you're screwed.

Always remember that the worldview of progressives, though many are sincere, is based on the emotional attraction of their doctrine, rather than the track record of that doctrine in practice, empirical evidence, or facts. This is something the far-left leadership has counted on. Negrophiliac sensibilities, as with nearly all progressive ideology, *are based on emotional assessments.* That which is not—statistical evidence, for example—quite often will have been fabricated outright.

If you find yourself in conversation with people who may lean toward a progressive (negrophiliac) worldview, but who are nevertheless disposed to debate such issues intelligently, you might use the information here (or similar facts you have gleaned on your own) to neutralize their arguments and reinforce your position.

Racism is evil in all its forms, and negrophilia is no different. No, it is not as severe as Ku Klux Klan members lynching blacks, but it aids in gravitating our society toward one that promises to be every bit as soul-sick and liberty-stultifying as was segregationist America.

Conversation Piece: *Were you aware that Democratic president FDR's "New Deal" was passed conditionally, with the understanding that the federal government would ignore Klan violence?*

It is true that many Americans who practice negrophilia are simply misguided; however, we must remember that those dedicated political operatives who advance its principles are insincere at best, and malevolent at worst. In the case of the black politicians and activists I have mentioned, a better case cannot be made for the core similarities between people of all races: These men and women have proven themselves to be every bit as devious, avaricious, dishonest, self-seeking, craven, and racist as whites can be. In the future, it will strongly behoove Americans to seek out and support politicians who have courage enough to affirm the truths contained herein, to speak them without fear, and find security in the support of their constituents—whom they ought to be representing in the first place—*without equivocation.*

It is vital that career black activists, whom I affectionately refer to here as "poverty pimps," are ultimately marginalized to the degree that American white supremacist leaders have been marginalized. These parasites, who conspire to intellectually segregate Americans, and spiritually and economically pauperize black people, while advancing a dangerous and destructive social agenda, have suddenly become much more than activists: They have become an advance force, the first captains of the Thought Police. They continue to poison race relations in America, and are paving the way for those who would control every thought that Americans think, and every word they speak.

Lastly, white and black Americans who recognize negrophilia, political correctness, and other far-left devices for what they are *must* cultivate spines and resign themselves to being the objects of scorn and derision for a time. Resting on their sense of righteousness, and hoping against hope that the opposition will someday collapse under the weight of its own mendacity, is insane. It's like hoping a house fire will spontaneously put itself out. It is more than evident that those who perpetuate these evils have proven that they can successfully deceive enough Americans, black and otherwise, to implement their agenda. At this juncture, they are far more practiced at it than we are at neutralizing their deceptions. *Defeating them must carry the priority of repelling an invasion.*

I think it's glorious that my children are growing up in a country where it is all but impossible for them to conceptualize the manner of occurrences that transpired when I was their age, the experiences I had, and those (even more severe) of black people who went before me, as a result of others' bigotry. My kids just can't wrap their brains around the fact that when I was born there were still "Whites Only" and "Colored" signs in use in some parts of this nation. In certain significant ways, that's a good thing; it's also a good thing that they are being taught that these things did indeed occur. However, as with some concepts to which they are exposed on a regular basis, due to related devices of our socially engineered society (such as negrophilia), there are areas in which corrective measures are required on a regular basis. They are routinely surprised and occasionally amused at the difference between what they witness vis-à-vis real world interracial relations and diverse cultures, and what is presented to them by our society (in school, and in various media). I count them fortunate that they have authentic examples to appraise, versus somnambulistically and obediently accepting the counterfeit racial theory that's been ladled into Americans' cranial cavities for the past three decades. When you get right down to it, negrophilia is nothing more than the flip side of phrenology and other bigoted pseudo-sciences that Nazis and various white supremacist groups have used to "prove" the inferiority of nonwhite ethnic groups.

It's not white supremacy, but it's just as racist.

Conversation Piece: *I just read the other day that Birmingham, Alabama, public safety commissioner Bull Connor, the one who set dogs and fire hoses on civil-rights protestors—and whom activists like to compare Republicans and conservatives to—was a member of the Democratic National Committee and the Ku Klux Klan . . .*

Remember that negrophilia is a vehicle of the far left. It is not, and never has been, some sort of contrivance by which blacks are meant to "take over" America. For the designs of the far-left secular-socialists and Marxists, it is imperative that Americans become as culturally balkanized as possible—whites against blacks, gays against straights, men against women, rich against poor, immigrants against citizens—the more division, the better. The fact that many whites have adopted or affected certain aspects of "black culture" (for better or worse) is a trifle; despite the perception whites have been encouraged to assume, blacks are meant to remain largely ignorant, undereducated, and resentful, and perpetually so.

I remember a rather bizarre question I was occasionally asked by classmates when I was in grammar school. Someone would find out I was of mixed race and offer: "If the blacks and the whites had a war, whose side would you be on?"

The apparent absurdity of this query obviously stems from the fact that it was typically asked by six-to-ten-year-olds, who normally have a tendency to look at these abstracts rather superficially. Still, there's something about this recollection that brings to mind the current state of race relations and race politics.

There's a war on right now—not just in the Middle East, or on terrorism, but on the home front—for the hearts and minds of Americans. No longer is it a question of what's good for America versus what's not so good for America—it's a question of what might ensure America's survival versus what will most assuredly destroy this nation.

Hard-left progressives—who are a minority—are nevertheless a strategically placed and highly vocal minority whose influence is inordinately potent. That they espouse policies which weaken America is, to many of us, a given. With lines becoming more clearly drawn every day, it is becoming increasingly important for ethnic minorities to become enlightened as to the stakes involved in this war, how they are being manipulated, and what is truly in their best interest.

Some blacks, individuals of other ethnic minorities, and white progressives presume that people like me are wholly insensitive to—and ignorant of—many issues regarding race. Based on the rhetoric I hear directed at us, we've obviously never suffered the effects of prejudice; never been sub-jected to name-calling; have somehow avoided bigotry in schools, the work-place, and in housing; and certainly never, ever had to fight over race, or flee for our lives from people who sought to harm or even kill us because of our skin color. We grew up in idyllic, color-blind enclaves, were nurtured perfectly and lovingly, attended the best prep schools and Ivy League uni-versities, sailed triumphantly into the job market through the connections of our color-blind white pals, and have been living large ever since.

At best, we're misguided and clueless; at worst, we're sellouts and race traitors. Why? Because we refuse to mindlessly follow those self-appointed career activists who rail against the U.S. as a "racist nation" (as though blacks still had to fear being lynched in the streets), and who continue to support the same programs that have not only failed for nearly half a century, but which have debased minorities to a degree unimaginable fifty years ago, and which would do an old Jim Crow supporter proud.

With respect to these detractors: In no way do I consider myself obliged to enumerate or detail the countless instances of racism and discrimination I have experienced, although they were by no means as severe as those suffered by blacks a generation ahead of me. In my view, black Americans who believe as I do should in no manner feel compelled to validate themselves or their positions to rapacious activ-ists, or brainwashed, arrogant joiners, who have nothing to offer but empty, parroted platitudes. The *last* ones to whom they ought to con-sider justifying themselves is the new generation of race-baiters who have no frame of reference for dealing with bigots, discrimination, or what racism even looks like, let alone *feels* like.

Conversation Piece: *Did you know that a lot of the resistance and opposition Jack Kennedy faced as president came from within his own party, the Democrats, because he favored civil-rights legislation and desegregation?*

It is the professional minority civil-rights activist who is the faceless racist in a suit, actively trying to keep those of his own ethnic group down. It is the elite progressive power broker, bent on implementing his twisted vision, who continues to advance racist practices. I am convinced that if black Americans came to a sudden, revelatory understanding of what these people have done to them, they would take to the streets with torches and pitchforks; there would be nowhere to hide.

The same parties who supported segregation simply modified their modus operandi as civil-rights laws were passed; blacks remained enslaved through entitlements rather than oppressive laws. Now, under the "big umbrella" of the political left, they are being sold into the slavery of socialism. Of course, we all are, but among minorities, the left's vehicle is the promulgation of petty issues, mistrust, and class envy. As they undermine race relations, they also deflect concern from the real dangers Americans face, among which is the political left itself.

As far as race relations and race politics goes, if you take anything away from this book, let it be this: For all practical purposes, there are no races anymore. In America, there are freedom fighters and there are those who would enslave all of us, regardless of race—and it's time to choose a side.

afterword

I T MAY BE a somewhat surprising and greatly sobering revelation
to some Americans that individuals perceived to be of as disparate
philosophies as President Obama and former President George W.
Bush have both bought into progressivism. While one's vision is more
toward the left (or the right) than the other, they, as well as countless
other powerful people, share the notion that middle-class people in
the West will have to accept socioeconomic retrogression and a fundamental stultification of their liberties under the pretext of promoting peace, global unity, and bringing the third world into the Bronze
Age. These folks will remain in the lap of luxury, but if the reader has
learned anything over the last generation or so, that won't be anything new. The worldview of these power brokers is an oligarchical
one that appeals only to narcissists.

Many Americans, perhaps even most, are quite spoiled. It is not
enough to have been born in a nation possessing the greatest measure of opportunity on the planet; Americans have been quick to buy
into the culture of class envy advanced by progressives. In this, black
Americans are no exception. For many, no compensation or restitution will ever be good enough to counterbalance past evils; in the case

of the activists among them, of course, if the job is ever done, then so are they. It is true that the minds of many black Americans have been poisoned, but in the end, we all must be accountable for our actions.

If we can rouse enough of our fellows to stifle the momentum of our domestic enemies, America may yet be able to hold on long enough to reaffirm constitutional preeminence, and people of every ethnic background will have an opportunity to thrive. The fact that the rest of the socialized Western world will balk at our doing so should be of no concern whatever to the American people, *because our way is indeed superior to theirs.* It has been proven again and again.

Most of what I have included in this book is a matter of historical record. For the rest, all it takes is a little critical thinking to see its truth. Unfortunately, blacks in America have been encouraged *not* to employ critical thinking; most of those who possess an education have been indoctrinated into far-left dogma, and those who do not are locked in socioeconomic and psychological squalor. Sadly, some of the former aid in keeping the latter where they are.

Black Americans have been a key pillar of the progressives' base for a long time, so if this book goes any distance at all toward dislodging that pillar and ultimately collapsing the structure, I will have done my job.

notes

[1] Paul Johnson, *A History of the American People* (New York: HarperCollins, 1997), 8.

[2] Ibid., 9.

[3] Jeffrey Lord, "The Democrats' Missing History," *Wall Street Journal*, August 13, 2008.

[4] Mark Galli, "Defeating the Conspiracy: Ignorance, Prejudice, and Even Bible Christianity Joined Forces to Sabotage the Faith of African-American Slaves," *Christianity Today*, April, 1999.

[5] The Sentencing Project, "New Incarceration Figures: Thirty-Three Consecutive Years of Growth," www.sentencingproject.org.

[6] Heather MacDonald, "Is the Criminal-Justice System Racist?" *City Journal*, Spring 2008.

[7] Child Trends, "High School Dropout Rates," October 2005, www.childtrendsdatabank.org.

[8] Ibid.

[9] Stan J. Liebowitz, "The Real Scandal: How Feds Invited the Mortgage Mess," *New York Post*, February 5, 2008.

[10] Jerome R. Corsi, "The Criminal Case Against ACORN," *WorldNetDaily*, July 24, 2009.

index

index

They come from the fields, and towns, and cities.

Sophisticates and the common.

They come to the power centers, exactly like their ancestors two centuries ago.

When American intuition tells the citizens that government by the people and for the people is being threatened... they come to make their voices heard!

In this tribute to that spirit of America, *Don't Tread on US!* offers a pictorial record of the new tea parties and their participants: classic signs that communicate most effectively with our brethren all across the land who oppose what's going on in Washington today. With a radical health-care agenda being marched across open territory, those citizens — tens of millions of them — are rallying, and will make their voices heard.

The colonial heart still beats today, and the people have spoken: ***Don't Tread on US!***

WND Books

WND Books • A WorldNetDaily Company • Washington, DC • www.DontTreadOnUS.com

Dangerous winds are blowing across America's culture today,
creating an atmosphere of extreme anxiety.

So why is the government making things worse?

Former TV meteorologist turned talk show host Brian Sussman wondered that for years,
and a decade's worth of investigation has yielded one of the most shocking stories of our time.

CLIMATEGATE

A VETERAN METEOROLOGIST
EXPOSES THE GLOBAL WARMING SCAM

BY BRIAN SUSSMAN

WND BOOKS™

WND Books   •   A WorldNetDaily Company   •   Washington, DC   •   www.wndbooks.com